# The
# Virginia Bentley Cookbook

By Virginia Bentley

*Let Herbs Do It*
*Bentley Farm Cookbook*
*The Virginia Bentley Cookbook*

# The
# Virginia Bentley
# Cookbook

More Great Recipes from
the Author of the
*Bentley Farm Cookbook*

by
## Virginia Bentley

Drawings by
Virginia Hoyt Cantarella

Houghton Mifflin Company
Boston · 1987

Library of Congress Cataloging-in-Publication Data

Bentley, Virginia Williams.
The Virginia Bentley cookbook.

Includes index.
1. Cookery.   I. Title.
TX715.B4818   1987      641.5973      86-27513
ISBN 0-395-42861-0
ISBN 0-395-42862-9 (pbk.)

Printed in the United States of America

V 10 9 8 7 6 5 4 3 2 1

The author is grateful to Stanley J. Sharpless for permission
to reprint his poem "In Praise of Cocoa, Cupid's Nightcap."

— To Judy and Dave,
whose homemaking and hospitable propensities
delight my soul —

# Contents

# Introduction

"I don't like to say that my kitchen is a religious place, but I would say that if I were a voodoo princess I would conduct my rituals there."
Pearl Bailey

I'm with you, Pearl. You've said it all.

Going from a large farm kitchen to a small one in a condominium has not broken the spell of fascination with the creativity of cooking. My love of that art seems not to have abated but intensified with age. And if going from large to small had its traumatic moments, I was sustained by the memory of the minuscule kitchens on dining cars in the great days of railroading. Output of of fine food has little relation to kitchen size.

It has been eleven years since my last cookbook effort, seven of them spent in the South, where great cooks abound, and my repertoire of recipes was thereby enriched. To borrow a phrase from Anne Morrow Lindbergh, I can say, "Thank you for stretching my heart out of its New England shell." To know the South is to love it, Arkansas in particular. Like the Biblical Jacob, I have found seven-year phases to have had undue significance in my life and, like Jacob, I've returned to the land of my roots much benefited by the experiences of far places.

People often asked me (to be polite and make

conversation, though I sometimes detected a glazed look around the eyes) when I was going to write another cookbook. My unfortunate answer was, "One needs to be a widow to write about cooking. I'm too busy getting three squares a day to put anything down on paper." Casual comment having become self-fulfilling prophecy, here I am, alone once more and back in New England, though not at the farm whose enchantment was mine for thirty-five years and will ever be my spiritual home. Maya Angelou has expressed it perfectly: "I've always said you can't go home again for the simple reason that one never leaves it. You take it with you everywhere you go."

As for the above-mentioned glazed look, I must face the fact that some people do not find the subject of eating as fascinating as I do. That seems strange to me, for as Talleyrand so delightfully inquired, "Can you inform me of any other pleasure which can be enjoyed three times a day, and equally in old age as in youth?"

Being a firm believer that work is more fun than play, that cooking is coping and joy-giving and love-giving, even life-giving, I figure it is time to get my eleven years' heap of recipes in order, and that adds up to another book.

The question most often asked now is, "What is the emphasis of your new book?" A good question. We are all aware of the staggering array of cookbooks that pour off the presses each year. Hasn't the last word been said? Indeed not. Cooking is infinite in its variations. As to what is the emphasis, here goes: more vegetables and fruits, less fat and sugar, ease of preparation, use of ingredients available at any supermarket, cooking healthfully without being a zealot. There's emphasis on good old down-to-earth American cooking, for so much of it is being lost under an avalanche of ethnic cookbooks — which are great, but so are our distinctly U.S. recipes. Cooking has become international in this country to a degree that is amazing, a natural result of massive immigration and a wide-traveling public. So I'm highlighting some old-time favorites that, to a younger generation, seem new.

This is not a definitive cookbook in any sense. (I assume that everyone has at least two of such. Mine are Fannie Farmer and Joy of Cooking, the first things I'd grab in case of fire. And, of course, I'd rescue my two: Let Herbs Do It and Bentley Farm Cookbook.) My hope is that I've gathered recipes that are as appealing as they are simple to prepare and will make the reader want to try them, to think, "That's a cinch; I can do that; guess I'll have a party." Inviting people to one's home is the surest antidote to the doldrums, whether it's to share a cup of tea and a cookie, a cocktail and an appetizer, or a full-course meal. The preparation of food has been an organizing force since the beginning of time, and the surest way to leave life's mainstream is to cease such activity.

You'll find in this book an emphasis on basic ingredients like cider vinegar, corn oil, unbleached flour, real vanilla, real lemons, butter. (You can, of course, use margarine. It won't taste as good, but go ahead. What your mind thinks is good for you may be more important than taste. My mind thinks that by drinking fat-free milk I can, like the Biblical Jael, "bring forth butter in a lordly dish".) Butter is a great, natural food. When I read the label on a package of margarine, I wonder how all those strange ingredients can possibly be better for one and keep hoping it's a fad that doctors will eventually advise against, like leeching. There are times when I'd rather eat a little of what's good than a lot of what's good for me.

I must confess to using canned soups in many recipes; nor do I make my own mayonnaise. Hellmans and Cains seem to taste better. But the mind-boggling arrays of bottled salad dressings and cake and cookie and muffin mixes and such never find their way into my grocery cart. I find it about as easy to cook from scratch with fresh, honest ingredients. Goodness knows how long the boxes have aged on the shelves, and the list of additives therein scares me off. The few times I've been overcome with inertia and bought myself a T.V. dinner, I've found standing next to me at the check-out counter some shocked acquaintance whose opinion of me as a dedicated cook has taken a noticeable plunge.

There's nothing more frustrating than finding

a good recipe in book or magazine that calls for exotic ingredients, or tiring procedures like clarifying broths or butter or frying in deep fat, or operations that soil innumerable cooking utensils. I automatically eliminate them from consideration and have tried to do so in this book. If a recipe causes one to drive all over town for truffle juice or Arborio rice or shiitake mushrooms (I'm definitely down on the last because they sound like Shiite Moslems), it won't be found in these pages. My salute to so-called "gourmet cooking" seems to be confined to grating whole nutmegs and grinding Tellicherry pepper.

All recipes in this book read from left to right, as one normally scans a page, rather than the ingredients being listed above and procedure below as in practically all printed recipes, inducing a yo-yo motion of head and eyes. (Speaking of eyes, people tell me they can read my large handwriting without glasses.) Ingredients are listed in order used and, where possible, dry measuring before wet, to save dishes. Extensive use of underlining is to help you grasp ingredients and functions of a recipe at a glance.

With so many women working outside their

homes these days, there's a need for quick recipes and dishes that can be prepared ahead of time for entertaining. I've had these miracle women (and men!) who manage to run homes as well as jobs very much in mind. There's a raft of good eating in simple preparations. "Good, good for you, and easy to prepare" is still my theme song. I sang it in the first <u>Bentley Farm Cookbook</u> that contains so many of my basic favorites, and I sing it again in this collection which is comprised of all new and different recipes.

As is evident, many recipes herein have been given me by kind friends, which is the nicest way there is to build up a meaningful collection. To each and every generous donor — my heartfelt thanks. I've become especially fascinated by friends who claim they are poor cooks. From such over-modest people I've gotten some of the best recipes. One friend denigrated herself so completely and in a remark so classic I have to share it. She (the mother of six healthy young people) said, "I'm such a terrible cook that when my kids went away to school they loved the food."

The purpose of this book will be fulfilled if it helps parents (or anyone) to head for the kitchen with more anticipation than dread and causes the kids to be devotees of home cooking.

# Beverages ∽ Appetizers ∽ Sandwiches

## About Beverages

Drinking habits seem to have changed drastically in the last score of years, more wine drinking and less hard liquor, and often just "water on the rocks." Tastes are so varied that when inviting people just _for cocktails_ I set up an area for drinks that _run_ the gamut: Perrier water, ginger ale, wine (mostly white wine for the young), beer, vodka, gin, bourbon, Scotch, rye (rarely called for but sometimes one who wants it) tonic water, club soda, a pitcher of water—and the table begins to groan. The sideboard always has its decanters of sherry and Dubonnet, so almost any taste can be satisfied. Add to all this plenty of ice, appropriate drink glasses, cocktail napkins, a corkscrew and bottle opener, a lemon, sharp knife and clean dish towel for spills and the spread is ready for anyone to take over. Let it be a self service affair. This seems to make everyone happy and the only work involved is getting everything out before the party and putting it away afterward, but that gets to be routine. Several men who are good at bartending usually take over, so the hostess can relax. It's only necessary to keep a weather eye out for any signals from the bar that some little thing is needed.

If entertaining at a dinner party it is helpful to have two wine coasters with the wine bottle in one and a carafe of some non-alcoholic beverage in another. (See suggestions page 5 ). Let guests help themselves unless there's an enthusiastic pourer in the group or the unheard of luxury of a maid!

After-dinner liqueurs are not as popular as they once were. In case you want to serve them, it's helpful to have a tray on some side table all set up with the bottles of your choice and the tiny glasses ready. No last minute clutching at a time when you may be running out of steam.

When it comes to beverages for all sorts of social gatherings such as a morning coffee, afternoon tea, etc., a variety of suggestions are to be found on some of the following pages.

# Banana Frappé (It's worth having a blender just for this one recipe.)

This happens to be my own invention. Try it! Your life will take on new dimensions (but not your figure). It's a mostly fat-free delectable health drink, a meal in itself, rich in potassium. Bananas have a way of ripening all at once and there's a limit to the amount of banana bread one can make or consume. So, peel your totally ripe bananas and wrap separately in plastic wrap and store in the freezer. I'm never without frozen ripe bananas.

Into your blender toss:

1 frozen banana, cut into a few pieces  
1 cup skimmed milk  
1 raw egg (optional but nourishing)  
vanilla — a good splash  
maple syrup — only a touch (consult your conscience)  
nutmeg — a generous sprinkling. (Best grated fresh, but any ground nutmeg will do.)

Blend thoroughly, pour into tall glass and enjoy.

This drink has the quality of an ice cream frappé due to the ice cold banana that thickens the whole. I get an enormous lift from it. Could it be the nutmeg that Malcolm X claimed he used when he couldn't get hard drugs? He wrote that it was possible to "take a trip" on nutmeg. I'm joking — even if he was not. This makes an ideal breakfast or lunch when one is hurried and takes only seconds to concoct. And it would make an invalid take up his bed and walk.

Sue Loomis's     <u>Pink Frappé</u>    (serves 4)

½ cup orange juice
2 cups cranberry juice    Put in blender.
1 cup vanilla ice cream   Blend well and
                    serve at once.

A refreshing summer afternoon drink that both
children and adults enthuse over. Don't forget
a plate of cookies.

<u>Suggestions for non-alcoholic drinks
to be served at table</u>:

① <u>Ginger ale</u> and <u>cranberry juice</u>, half and half,
        when a rosé wine is served.

② <u>Plain ginger ale</u> with champagne.

③ <u>White grape juice</u> with any white wine.

④ <u>Concord grape juice</u> with a red wine.

      These are my four standbys which I serve
in carafes to match whatever wine is being
served. Non-drinkers find it merciful. So do
children who love to have something to drink
from a wine glass.

# Cocoa (serves 6)

4 tablespoons cocoa (unsweetened)
2 tablespoons sugar (or more, to taste)
sprinkle of salt
4 cups milk (1 quart) (I use fat-free)
few drops of vanilla

Toss all into blender and whirl away until well mixed. Transfer to double boiler and heat.

- - - - - - - - -

You may top with a marshmallow or some whipped cream but that is optional. A soothing, satisfying winter drink.

Cocoa, to me, always demands one of three things as a partner:

① A toasted English muffin, generously buttered.
I'll never forget that combination as served at Schrafft's in Boston when I was young and the word "cholesterol" unheard of. The butter ran up my wrist. The whipped cream gave me a lovely white mustache.

② Cinnamon toast — This was our Sunday night supper, always, throughout my youth. Our large Sunday breakfasts and noontime dinners called for an evening halt.

③ A chicken sandwich on homemade white bread with butter, mayonnaise and Boston lettuce. The Brockton Club in Brockton, Mass., the old shoe factory town, made a chicken sandwich that has never been excelled. My father, who was in the leather business, had to go to Brockton often. On special occasions we kids were allowed to go along for the ride in his wonderful open Chalmers car, lunching at the club on that heavenly combination of chicken sandwich and cocoa.

You can, of course, buy instant cocoa, but

I avoid it not only because its not as good but its one more container to overcrowd the kitchen cupboard. And basic cocoa can be used for many other purposes. Should you not be up to making cocoa from scratch, here's an easy way out: Buy chocolate milk and heat it.

Here's a poem "in praise of cocoa, cupid's nightcap" by Stanley J. Sharpless, "written upon hearing the startling news that cocoa is a mild aphrodisiac":

Half past nine — high time for supper;
"Cocoa, love?" "Of course, my dear."
Helen thinks it quite delicious,
John prefers it now to beer.
Knocking back the sepia potion,
Hubby winks, says, "Who's for bed?"
"Shan't be long", says Helen softly,
Cheeks a faintly flushing red.
For they've stumbled on the secret
Of a love that never wanes,
Rapt beneath the tumbled bedclothes,
Cocoa coursing through their veins.

8

## Ethel's Daffodil Punch   (easy and different)

apricot nectar   ) approximately equal parts of each, and for
pineapple juice ) every quart of punch add:

2 teaspoons vanilla

Pour over ice and that's it.

~~~~~~~~~~

## Summer Punch  (serves 6 or 8)

(As served by Happy Griffith in her delightful garden, where herbs
and vegetables and flowers in abundance created a magic world apart.)

2 cups mint leaves that have been well crushed, muddled, packed down.
2 cups boiling water, poured over mint leaves. Let steep 2 hours.
1 pint white or red grape juice, to which the mint tea is added.
simple syrup, to taste (1 part sugar to 2 parts water brought to boil
   and cooled.)
1 pint ginger ale, added just before serving over plenty
                                              of ice.

This recipe may be multiplied
   endlessly for a crowd!.
(Mint leaves are, of course, strained out of tea after steeping.)

~~~~~~~~~~

# Mulled Cider (serves 8)

½ gallon (2 quarts) apple cider
several sticks of cinnamon
a few cloves

Heat slowly to draw out the spicy flavor. Do not boil.

Should you have an urge to be fancy, peel some navel oranges, round and round, stud the spirals with a few cloves and place a curl in each mug, or several in a punch bowl.

(Serve orange sections alone or with bananas or any fruit for your next meal to use up the precious peeled oranges.)

# Christmas Punch (serves 8)

2 quarts cranberry juice

1 cup seedless raisins

⅓ cup chopped candied orange peel

½ cup blanched almonds

2 sticks cinnamon

1 teaspoon whole allspice

10 cloves

½ teaspoon almond extract

Heat all this slowly in non-metal kettle. Don't hurry it. You want to draw out the flavors. Ladle into cups with all the embellishments except the two cinnamon sticks.
Top each serving with

lemon slices that have had a clove or two pressed into them.

## Sudden Death (serves 30 or more, depending on thirst.)

Always served on New Year's Day at the hospitable home of Mabel and Jack Barr in Stewartsville, New Jersey. I can't allow this recipe to be assigned to oblivion. It gave too many people so much fun through the years. Here's the way Mabel did it:

6 teaspoons black tea
6 teaspoons green tea
} Pour 1 quart boiling water over tea. Steep about 10 minutes. Strain off tea into adequate-sized container and add:

juice of 12 lemons
6 of the lemon rinds
} Cover. Allow to stand several hours or overnight. When ready to make the punch, remove rinds and pour tea into punch bowl.
Add:

½ cup sugar
1 quart gin
2 quarts dark Jamaica rum
} Stir well. Add a block of ice and, last of all, stir in:

1 quart carbonated water (club soda)
1 quart orange juice

Happy New Year!

# Russian Tea  (Serves 30)

This is not only a treat to have on hand for one's self but a splendid concoction for gift-giving in an attractive jar. Remember to include directions for serving.

1 cup instant unsweetened tea
   (Use decaffeinated if you prefer.)
1 cup sugar (or less, according to taste)
2 cups Tang powdered orange drink
½ cup lemonade mix
1 teaspoon cinnamon
½ teaspoon ground cloves

Mix thoroughly. Put into one large jar or several small ones with tight lids.

Use 1 tablespoon of Russian Tea per cup of boiling water.

It's doubtful that any real Russians ever quaffed this blend, but they just might be pleased if they did.

## Sun Tea

This is the greatest for summer living when one wants iced tea on hand at all hours:

Fill a glass jar with cold water. Then place tea bags in the jar — one bag to each cup of water. Place the jar, covered, outdoors in the sun for several hours. There are no hard and fast rules concerning time. This produces a good, strong, clear, non-bitter tea — all set to keep in the refrigerator and pour over ice when needed. It keeps for days.

I've been known to forget the sunning jar and have left it out overnight — apparently not to the detriment of this fine infusion.

Herb teas may be made this way, too. And loose teas may be used as well as tea bags: one teaspoon of tea to a cup of water.

# About Appetizers

If you are serving something for the cocktail hour before a dinner party, make it simple, dainty, almost stingy. It's a great mistake to fill up guests on rich canapés before a fine meal. One hot hors d'oeuvre is enough, with maybe one cold one such as some nuts or finger greens or crackers and cheese. Things that are all prepared to pop in one's mouth are preferable for the cocktail hour, when one is usually seated! Appetizers that need to be dipped, spread, worked over, are more appreciated at a cocktail party, where one is walking around. Perhaps the most important thing to say about the "happy hour" before dinner is to keep it as near to an hour as possible. Otherwise don't bother to prepare a lovely meal. Guests are pretty well beyond appreciation if they've been snacking and imbibing for two or three hours. There's a fine line between gracious living and running hospitality into the ground. Try to follow the fine line.

Cocktail parties are another matter. Their long-lastingness is usually the mark of success. And when it comes to appetizers, serve all the variety and quantity you have the energy to muster. Only one suggestion: When serving finger greens, which are always welcomed, cut them into bite-sized pieces. If too large, guests are forced into the unsanitary habit of eating the part with the dip on it and then having to dip again. (Is that being too fussy?!) An array of goodies follows that I hope will inspire you to call in the neighbors right away.

Nancy Sawyer's     Artichoke Dip (This disappears so fast
that its impossible to
say how many it
will serve.)

2 cans artichoke hearts, 8 ½ ounces each, artichokes in water,
not marinated. Drain well. Cut up
thoroughly.

1 cup mayonnaise

1 teaspoon garlic powder

1 cup grated Parmesan cheese

　　　　　Mix all of above. Place in attractive
baking dish. Bake in preheated
350° oven 20 or 30 minutes until
browned and bubbly.
Serve with

Tortilla chips — for dipping.

Martha Purdy's   <u>Artichoke Quiche Appetizers</u> (serves 8 or more)

They freeze well. A great do-ahead.

<u>2 jars marinated artichoke hearts</u> (6 ounces each), drained and
      chopped, saving half the oil in one jar
      in which to sauté

<u>1 onion</u>, finely chopped. Sauté in pan large enough for whole recipe.
      When onion is soft, remove pan from heat. Allow
      to cool somewhat before adding all the following:

<u>4 beaten eggs</u>
<u>¼ teaspoon garlic salt</u>
<u>¼ teaspoon oregano</u>
<u>¼ cup bread crumbs</u>
<u>Tabasco</u>, several gentle shakes
<u>freshly grated pepper</u>
<u>2 tablespoons dried parsley flakes</u> (or triple if chopped fresh)
<u>½ pound sharp Cheddar cheese</u>, grated

      Pour all into buttered 9" x 13" pan.
      Bake in preheated <u>350° oven</u> for ½ hour.
      Cool and cut into 1 inch squares.
      Reheat when ready to serve.

No one ever served better food than Martha!
I cherish this recipe.

## Caviar Pie (Serves 10 to 12)
(This is always a hit. Thank you, Jean Tyson.)

6 hard boiled eggs, chopped fine ⎫ Mix and spread in bottom of
3 tablespoons mayonnaise ⎭ a non-metal 9" pie plate. (I use Corning ware.)

1½ cups finely chopped onion, spread over above.
 (one big Bermuda onion is about right but any onion will do.)

⅔ cup sour cream ⎫ Mix well and layer over
8-ounce package cream cheese, softened ⎭ the onion with wet knife.

4-ounce jar black caviar, spread over all. Chill for a good 3 hours or overnight. When ready to serve, place caviar pie on a larger plate or tray and surround with squares of
Melba toast (page 27) and
lemon wedges — plenty of them — to squeeze over every bite.

(Eggs and then onions, separately, are easily chopped in food processor if you have one. Also, you may double the amount of caviar if in a lavish mood but four ounces are enough for me.)

Marmie's  **Baked Chicken Bit Dips** (serves 8 or 10 for cocktails.)

2 whole chicken breasts (4 halves), boned, skinned, cut into
bite-sized pieces, and tossed in melted butter.

⅓ cup grated Parmesan cheese
1 teaspoon salt
1 teaspoon dried basil
1 teaspoon dried thyme
¾ cup fine bread crumbs *

Put all this together in paper or plastic bag and shake well. Then add chicken pieces, a few at a time, and shake some more to coat them well. Arrange chicken bits on oiled cookie sheet. (Butter smokes too much in a hot oven.) When ready to serve, bake in preheated 400° oven, top shelf, for 10 minutes or until nicely browned.

Sauce for Dipping:

¾ cup mayonnaise
2 heaping tablespoons honey  } Beat together thoroughly.

~~~~~~~~~~~~~~~~~

I've been known to cut the chicken in larger pieces and serve for a plate luncheon with a bit of the dip drizzled thereon, Fondue Tomatoes (page 196), and rice.

~~~~~~~~~~~~~~~~~

* A food processor is perfect for making crumbs. Use up stale bread this way and have crumbs ever ready in a screw-top jar in refrigerator.

~~~~~~~~~~~~~~~~~

# Three-Way Crab Dish

1. Serve for cocktails with plain melba toast (page 27).
2. Serve as main luncheon dish.
3. Spread on bread for hot open sandwiches.

(Crabmeat — fresh is best but canned will do.
8 ounces (½ pound) Chop fine for canapés.

3 ounces cream cheese, softened
⅓ cup mayonnaise
⅓ cup sour cream
½ cup grated Parmesan cheese
1 medium onion, finely chopped
Worcestershire Sauce — a dash
1 teaspoon prepared horseradish
1 teaspoon prepared mustard
salt and pepper — a touch

Mix all this together thoroughly. Then add the crabmeat. Put into buttered baking dish. Bake uncovered in preheated 350° oven for 30 minutes or more, or until slightly tanned and bubbly.

1. This will serve 12 for cocktails.
2. It should serve 4 to 6 for lunch.
3. I've made open sandwiches from leftovers of this dish and placed them on a cookie sheet and baked in preheated 400° oven so the bread browns on the bottom and the crab mixture browns a bit on top. If you started from scratch with the fresh mixture, it would make 8 generous open sandwiches. And make 8 people very happy.

# Cucumber Canapés or Tea Sandwiches

These are special favorites with me because the ingredients are ever at hand and they look so fancy and they're really not. And they are universally popular.

cucumber ⎫ Cut as many slices of cucumber as you need.
bread ⎭ Cut an equal number of circles of bread. Then cut the cucumber slices to match. This removes the skin.

cream cheese, softened
mayonnaise, enough to make mixture spreadable ⎫ Mix this together well until satisfactorily
dill weed (dried or chopped fresh), added with heavy hand ⎬ spreadable. Spread on each bread round and
Sidney's Herb Mix ★ (page 286), according to taste ⎭ top with cucumber. Garnish with . . . . .
(optional but good)

paprika — just a pinch in center of each cucumber, for color.

You'll need a round sharp cutter for above operation. I'm blessed with a tin box of these in graduated sizes. They are really cookie cutters and pictured in most kitchen catalogues. Lacking this gadget, just cut your bread in squares, score the cucumber with a sharp fork and then slice the cucumber. It will have a pretty serrated effect and be "sitting pretty" on a square rather than a circle. Time saving too.

For a truly glamorous hors d'oeuvre : Skewer a shrimp atop above cucumber sandwich with a toothpick. This is gilding the lily a bit, but why not? Shrimp and cucumber and dill are soul mates.

★ If you haven't gotten around to making Sidney's Mix, substitute some salt.

Jean Rowland's  <u>Cheese Wafers</u> (makes at least 50)

1 cup shredded sharp Cheddar cheese
1 tablespoon Parmesan cheese, grated
1 stick butter (¼ pound), softened
¼ teaspoon salt
a few drops Tabasco and/or Worcestershire Sauce

1 cup flour
¼ cup sesame seeds
1 cup Rice Krispies

Mix in order given. Refrigerate an hour or more to facilitate handling. Form into small balls. Place on buttered cookie sheet. Flatten with fork. Bake in preheated 350° oven for 10 or 12 minutes until golden. Watch! Great will be your reward.

## Onion Canapés

This is similar to Gen's Dip (page 23) but a bit different in that the onion is in evidence, its not served as dip, and can be produced in minutes for any emergency. No need to run to the grocery store as all ingredients are standard supplies in most homes.)

*chopping some parsley with the onion is optional but oh-so-good.*

① Mix Parmesan cheese and mayonnaise, half and half.

② Spread on bread from which crusts have been removed.

③ Press finely chopped onion onto each slice.

④ Cut into squares or fingers, place on cookie sheet and put in preheated 375° oven until slightly browned, about 5 minutes. Keep peeking.

# Gazpacho-Stuffed Cherry Tomatoes

Cherry tomatoes served whole and unadorned vie with water pistols in "squirtability." Here's a tasteful solution.

1 small cucumber, peeled, seeded, minced
¼ cup red bell pepper (or pimiento) minced
¼ cup green bell pepper, minced
1 small clove garlic, minced
1 Tablespoon red onion or scallions, minced

Mix, salt generously and put aside while preparing tomatoes. (Food processor makes this easy should you have one.)

1 pint (about 20) cherry tomatoes, small, bite-sized. Cut out stem ends and scoop out seeded center. Turn tomatoes upside down on paper towel to drain.

Now put the cucumber mixture in a strainer and press out all juice possible. Place in bowl and add:

2 teaspoons fresh lemon or lime juice
2 teaspoons olive oil or any good vegetable oil
1 Tablespoon chopped fresh mint leaves
      (or 1 heaping teaspoon dried mint)
pepper, to taste, salt if you must

Fill each tomato with this mixture and arrange them on serving dish that has been covered with a paper napkin or doily. (Otherwise tomatoes are given to sliding around) Finger greens placed between them are attractive and also keep the tasty bites under control.

# Two Easy Appetizers

① Spread softened cream cheese (in any amount you choose) over the bottom of an attractive pie plate.
Over the cheese, spread some ketchup in which you have mixed some horseradish.   Sprinkle the top with chopped crabmeat, fresh or canned.
Serve with Triscuits or Melba toast. Supply some butter knives for guests to spread their own.

This not only looks attractive, it tastes that way.

② Cut well-washed apples in quarters and core but do not peel. Cut each quarter into 3 or 4 pieces and drop immediately into a bowl of water to which you have added the juice of a lemon and a touch of salt. (This treatment keeps apples from turning brown.) Refrigerate until ready to serve when apples should be patted dry with paper towels. Arrange slices attractively interspersed with bite-sized pieces of cheese.   (This appetizer also makes a fine dessert.)

## Jen's Dip

(Of the many cocktail party recipes I've gathered in the past ten years — this takes the blue ribbon.)

1 cup mayonnaise
1 cup grated sharp Cheddar
1 good-sized onion, grated

} Mix and put into baking dish. (I use a small soufflé dish.) Hold until ready to serve. Then bake in preheated 400° oven for 15 minutes. It puffs and browns temptingly.

Serve at once with tortilla chips or melba toast or raw vegetables. Guests have a way of ignoring anything else you may provide.

If you have a food processor, the cheese and onion are more easily prepared in it. (But don't make a mush! Let it be rather coarse-textured.)

Should there be any of Jen's Dip left over, use it to make a toasted cheese sandwich another day.

# Gougère (according to Betty Hagen)

Gougère is also called Burgundian Pastry and is said to have originated in Sens. Anyway, its a cross between Yorkshire Pudding and popovers and better than either and easier to produce. It may be made with Swiss, Gruyère or Cheddar cheese.

1 cup milk
¼ cup butter (½ a quarter pound stick)
½ teaspoon salt
freshly ground pepper (be generous)

} Combine in saucepan and bring to a boil. Remove from heat and add all at once:

⅞ cup flour (all purpose unbleached) Stir vigorously. Return to heat, stirring until mixture comes away from sides of pan. Remove from heat and add:

3 eggs — one at a time, stirring hard.

1 tablespoon cream or milk
¼ pound grated cheese (I prefer sharpest Cheddar)

} Stir into above. Put dough into buttered, shallow baking dish about 9 or 10 inches square or a generous pie plate.

1 egg, beaten and brushed over dough.

more grated cheese, sprinkled over the egg glaze.

Bake in preheated 400° oven for 15 minutes. Reduce heat to 350° and bake about another ½ hour or until puffed and brown. Serve hot or cold, cut into squares or wedges. You may also make cute little individual gougères by dropping small spoonfuls on oiled cookie sheet. (oiled rather than buttered so high heat will not cause smoking). Top each with egg and cheese, as above, and bake at 450° for 5 minutes, then 375° for about 15 minutes.

This is guaranteed to "wow" guests at a cocktail party. It is equally acceptable as the bread dish at a meal. No need to serve butter with it. It's complete in itself.

# Lobster Canapés

(20 bite-sized squares)

1 cup lobster meat,* chopped fine ⎫ (Food processor is handy but not vital.)
juice of ½ lemon ⎮ Mix and refrigerate. If it is a bit
1 bunch scallions, chopped ⎮ runny when ready to spread, press
(leaving on a little of the green) ⎮ out excess juice in a strainer.
mayonnaise - just enough to ⎮
bind together ⎮
salt and pepper - only a touch ⎭

5 thin slices of bread, crusts removed. Spread the lobster mixture thereon so bread is completely covered. Cut each slice into four squares and place on cookie sheet. Bake in preheated 350° oven until delicately toasted on the bottom (20 minutes or so). Serve warm.

One thing leads to another : Add some chopped celery to above recipe, toast and butter some hot dog rolls, make a small bed of shredded lettuce in the rolls and then fill with the lobster mixture. You now have a New England Lobster Roll — one of life's more delectable repasts.

* Lacking fresh-cooked lobster, get the canned frozen variety that comes from Canada. Its excellent! More than enough for this recipe and well worth the price.

# Cocktail Meatballs

(An Atlanta recipe)                    (60 to 80 small meatballs)

2 pounds lean ground beef  
¼ cup water  
1 onion, grated  
2 eggs, beaten  
1 cup cracker or bread crumbs  
1½ teaspoons salt  

} Mix well and shape into bite-sized meat balls.

1 one-pound can cranberry jelly  
1 twelve-ounce bottle chili sauce  
2 tablespoons brown sugar  
1 tablespoon lemon juice  

} Combine and bring to simmer in large pan, stirring often. Add meatballs carefully, cover and simmer 1½ hours or more. Beware of scorching. (This could be done in a slow oven; then no need to watch so carefully.)

This keeps warm a long while on cocktail table, but use some sort of warming device if you want: candle warmer, hot tray or chafing dish. Have toothpicks available for spearing plus small paper napkins to catch drips.

I've been known to serve this as a buffet supper dish, making the meatballs larger. It will serve 8.

The above type of recipe has been around for a long time, but this version is particularly toothsome and always popular.

# Melba Toast

There may be a passable variety of commercial melba toast but I have yet to find one. Its so easy to make yourself and so much better. Though any type of bread will do, I like the very thin-sliced Pepperidge white bread best. Cut into triangles, fingers or squares (with or without crusts) and dry out in a 250° oven until a delicate tan. It takes around an hour. Keep in airtight container.

The variations are numerous:

1. Butter the bread and then bake.
2. Mix butter and grated Parmesan and spread on bread.
3. Mix butter and any herb you desire to enhance whatever it is served with. For example: basil with tomato soup or salad; dill with fish chowder or fish salad. Variations are legion.
4. Butter mixed with Sidney's Herb Mix (page 286) is a favorite in our house. The house smells divine during the slow baking process. This served by itself makes a great cocktail snack and is a relief from the ubiquitous corn or potato chips.

Keeping melba toast on hand, in any form, answers the need for a hurry-up cocktail appetizer — as well as being an easier, more digestible and less fattening accompaniment to soups and salads than hot rolls.

Harriet Gundersen's <u>Plantation Hors d'Oeuvres</u> (serves 6)

<u>1 can Campbell's Consommé</u> (10½ ounces)

           Pour off 2 ounces of consommé and reserve.

           Pour remainder of consommé in blender.

<u>Scallions</u>, white part only of several —

       (enough to make about 1 tablespoon } Toss in blender.

           when chopped)

<u>1 teaspoon lemon juice</u>        Add to blender.

<u>½ teaspoon Worcestershire Sauce</u>    Blend well and pour into ramekins, punch cups, demitasse cups, or

<u>cream cheese</u> (8 ounces), cut in cubes } whatever and chill until set.

<u>1 tablespoon chopped fresh parsley</u>, sprinkled on the chilled

           and set hors d'oeuvres.

<u>remaining unjellied consommé</u>, spooned onto each. Then

           chilled again, thoroughly.


This is now ready to serve with cocktails on plates or saucers with small spoons and little fingers of Melba Toast (plain or herbed), or with dainty cheese wafers.

      I consider this one of the most treasured and unusual recipes in this book. It was one Charlotte Mahon's specialty. (The name "Plantation" suggests southern origins.) Thanks to Harriet Gundersen, the prize has been handed on to me. Enjoy!

Mary Kirk's    ## Pastrami Canapé   (Serves 8)

1 package pastrami (2.5 ounce), chopped )    A processor will
1 small can black olives (3.5 ounce), chopped )   do all this if you're
½ pound sharp Cheddar cheese, grated )   lucky enough to have one.

1 cup mayonnaise

        Mix all of above together and spread on
small party rye slices of bread . Place on foil-covered
        cookie sheet.
Put into preheated 400° oven and bake until bubbly, about
      15 minutes.

Thank you, Mary. These are always a hit.

## Speedy Vegetable Dip

1 eight-ounce package cream cheese , softened
1 bouillon cube (chicken or beef), dissolved in
½ cup boiling water

        Pour the hot bouillon over the cream cheese
and mix together thoroughly. Your dip
is ready for any finger greens you care
to prepare. This is not a rich dip as are
the sour cream and mayonnaise varieties.

# Shrimp

## How to Serve:

Shrimp are not only the most popular item at a cocktail party but also the most expensive (aside from imported black caviar). Arrange the precious things on a bowl of ice with toothpicks in them (if you have the time and ambition); otherwise have a container of toothpicks nearby. (A demitasse cup will serve the purpose, with its saucer a handy depository for used toothpicks.) The most attractive way I've ever seen shrimp served was in a giant sea shell resting on a bed of ice. Or scoop out a cabbage putting the Shrimp Sauce (recipe below) in the cavity and attaching shrimp all over the outside of the cabbage with toothpicks. I have a neighbor who serves several shrimp in punch cups, the shrimp skewered with toothpicks, the sauce all on them. Ever so efficient — guests needn't budge.

## How to Cook:

VERY LITTLE — 3 to 5 minutes is the maximum — and only until they turn pink. Don't cook shrimp at all if they are to be part of a cooked dish. Overcooked shrimp becomes tough and rubbery. Two pounds of shrimp yields a little over a pound after cooking and shelling. Depending on appetites and the type of recipe used, this peeled pound should serve about 4 to 6 people. For sheer luxury I like to order shrimp, all cooked, deveined and ready, from a good seafood store. When strength, time and an economy streak prevail, I cook them from scratch in the shell either in plain boiling salted water or in a Court Bouillon. You may take your choice of plain or fancy. (See next page.)

## Court Bouillon

Have enough _water_ in kettle so that shrimp will be covered. This recipe calls for about two pounds of shrimp.

1 onion, cut up, skin and all

2 tablespoons vinegar

1 carrot, cut up

1 rib celery and leaves, cut up

some parsley, dried or fresh

2 or 3 cloves

6 peppercorns

½ bay leaf

salt, a heaping teaspoon

Add all this to water, bring to a boil and allow to simmer a few minutes until pleasant odors are wafting about. Then toss the shrimp into the kettle. Bring to boil and simmer sparingly as directed on previous page. Drain at once. (Save the broth if you find it useful in some sauce.)

When shrimp are sufficiently cooled, remove shells and devein carefully. No one wants to eat that little black thread of digestive tract. It's harmless but unaesthetic. Some people remove shells before cooking. In that case add the shells to the cooking water. They make the shrimp more flavorful. Or you can buy frozen shrimp that are already shelled. Follow package directions. There are a dismaying array of choices these days. Chill shrimp rapidly after cooking and keep chilled on ice (if possible) as they are served. Serve with the following dip (none better):

## Shrimp Dip

1 cup Chili Sauce (not ketchup)

lemon juice from ½ a real lemon

1 heaping teaspoon horseradish

1 teaspoon Worcestershire Sauce

Mix and chill.

You may make a richer dip by stirring in some mayonnaise. I prefer it without.

# Spinach Balls   (Serves 6 or 8)

1 ten-ounce package frozen spinach ) Cook until just tender — no more.
  or                                  Drain thoroughly and either
1 pound fresh garden spinach ∫ chop well by hand or put into
                                     food processor.

2 tablespoons butter, added to hot spinach

¼ teaspoon garlic powder

¼ teaspoon dried thyme

salt and pepper, to taste

1 cup Pepperidge Farm Herb Stuffing

1 medium onion, chopped fine or added
                        to processor

Cheddar or Parmesan cheese, to taste,
      grated or added in pieces to food
           processor

All added to spinach in processor, or stirred in by hand, having first been finely chopped as indicated.

2 eggs, beaten, stirred into above and chilled.

The chilling makes it stiff enough to form into small balls. Place close together on well-buttered pan and bake in preheated 350° oven for 20 minutes.

Serve warm. They are easily picked up by hand as they are not greasy. Using a stove-to-table platter saves work. You may need a spatula to loosen them from the platter — but no problem. They adhere only ever so lightly. I like to make them in the morning and reheat quickly at cocktail time. They freeze well and recipe may be multiplied indefinitely for a crowd.

Stuffed Eggs (Bentley Farm Cookbook, page 123) and Lobster Canapés (this book, page 25) along with these Spinach Balls make a really smashing trio. Try it!

Sue Houle's  Spinach Dip  (serves 12 or more.)

2 ten-ounce packages frozen chopped spinach,
          thawed and well drained

1 envelope (1⅜ ounce) Knorr-Swiss Vegetable Soupmix

1 eight-ounce can water chestnuts, drained,
          chopped

1 cup mayonnaise

1 cup sour cream

Mix together and refrigerate for several hours. Overnight is better, for time improves the flavor.

This makes a thick dip, so serve with sturdy chips. You'll like its crunchiness.

# Zucchini Dip (low-cal)

1½ cups shredded zucchini, young, unpeeled.
Press out excess moisture in strainer. It will end up as about 1 cup.

1 cup plain yogurt
¼ cup mayonnaise
1½ tablespoons grated onion
1 teaspoon curry powder
salt, plain or garlic, to taste

Mix together well, then stir in the zucchini. Cover, refrigerate several hours to bring out the flavor.

Serve with vegetable sticks and/or chips of your choice.

---

Dorothy Atwell's     Chicken Liver Pâté     (serves 8)

¼ pound butter, melted in skillet. Pour off all but 2 tablespoons of the butter and reserve, keeping warm.
1 onion, cut up and sautéed lightly in the butter left in pan. Then add
1 pound best, fresh chicken livers and
1 clove garlic, minced

Cover. Cook about 5 minutes, stirring occasionally.

Now transfer all to food processor (or blender) along with reserved melted butter and
2 tablespoons brandy (or more) and
salt and pepper, to taste

Process well and pack into correct-sized attractive container or separate ramekins, according to need. Chill until ready to serve or freeze for storage.

Dorothy likes this better than fancy imported pâté. So do I!

---

# About Sandwiches

A sandwich can be one of life's great treats. A poorly made one is such an unnecessary disappointment as to make me plain angry.

A good sandwich must be made with high grade bread! With that the battle is half won. It should be spread right to the very edges with plenty of filling, yet not overdone to the point of squeezing out into one's lap. It must be free of all bones, fat, gristle, strings and other offensive inclusions. It should be moist without being runny, and well seasoned.

A disappointing sandwich usually advertises itself first by being made with cheap, cottony white bread with a stingy dab of filling in dead center only. Most bites are interrupted by removing something unpleasant you've bitten into. Then there are the soggy sandwiches, wet clean through and dripping their contents here and there. And the taste is always blah, devoid of imaginative seasoning.

Sandwich talk reminds me of the man who had to carry his lunch to work each day. Always groaning, he'd bring forth a plain peanut butter sandwich, eating away disconsolately. His co-workers grew tired of his daily complaints over the monotony of such fare and said, "Why on earth don't you ask your wife to make something different?" He replied, "I don't have a wife. I make my own lunch."

Here follow a few sandwich suggestions, some for lunch box or picnic, some better served at home.

The most valuable trick I've learned recently in sandwich-making comes from the Peter Christian Restaurant in Hanover, N.H. That is the use of cream cheese, which, spread on the inside of both top and bottom of a sandwich, gives a delicious richness, moisture, texture, yet coats the bread in such a way that it can't become soggy when the fillings are applied. Added to the cream cheese can be all sorts of seasonings—herbs, spices, grated vegetables, bouillon granules—to enhance the meat being used.

The possibilities are legion. (I can't imagine why I confined myself to using cream cheese only on a banana or nut bread sandwich.)

For a roast beef sandwich mix some horseradish into the cream cheese.
For chicken add a bit of tarragon and/or thyme.
For lamb add rosemary, garlic and lemon.
For cucumber or shrimp or crab or lobster add dill.
For ham mix in mustard and piccalilli.
For tomato some basil and/or oregano.

Mix Sidney's Herb Seasoning (page 286) with cream cheese.
    It will turn any sandwich into something
      exciting and unidentifiable.

Having suggested various herbs for sandwiches (and you are sure to think of some tasty variations of your own), I'd also like to warn against overuse of a good idea. Plain and simple tastes have a time-honored place, such as:

A BLT. (bacon, lettuce and tomato) on good toasted bread, well buttered, spread with mayonnaise, a touch of salt, pepper. This the sort of sandwich prepared at last minute and served at home. (This is one of my favorites and I admit to running it into the ground.)

Roast beef, well trimmed, on buttered bread with a touch of horseradish, mayonnaise and/or cold gravy, lettuce, salt and pepper.

Chicken on buttered bread with lettuce, mayonnaise, salt.

Lamb on buttered bread, some of its own gravy, salt and pepper.

Ham on buttered bread, mustard (a must), a slice of cheese, lettuce and mayonnaise.

~~~~~~~~~~

### Traditional Salad Sandwiches (All suitable for salads as well.)

(Make these sandwiches with cream cheese or not, according to your whim. )
(Traditionally one just spreads good bread with butter to the very edges and then proceeds.)

Chicken Salad Sandwich — chopped chicken (or turkey), celery, onion, green pepper, pimiento, olives, crumbled chicken bouillon cubes in place of salt. Bind with mayonnaise. Lettuce if you want.

Tuna Salad Sandwich — get best white tuna in water. Use some or all of chicken seasonings above.

Egg Salad Sandwich — chopped celery and onion, mustard, Worcestershire, a touch of ketchup and curry, salt, pepper, mayonnaise to bind. (A slice of ham added is special.) Lettuce maybe.

Shrimp, Crabmeat or Lobster Salad Sandwich — add chopped scallions and celery, dill, lemon juice or a touch of grated rind, salt and pepper to taste, mayonnaise. Lettuce.

Ham Salad Sandwich — chopped ham, piccalilli, mustard, mayonnaise. Dark bread, lettuce if you desire.

~~~~~~~~~~

Cream cheese does great things for sandwiches made with pumpernickel bread.   Mixing salt and pepper in the cheese assures a well-seasoned sandwich throughout.
If a sandwich spread appears too runny, press out liquid in strainer, or add cracker crumbs until consistency is suitable.

~~~~~~~~~~

# Satisfying Sandwich (for 4)

__4 onion rolls__, buttered, heated

__4 slices bologna__ , chopped
__4 hard-boiled eggs__, chopped
__1 rib celery__, chopped
__¼ cup sweet relish__
__¼ cup mayonnaise__
__1 teaspoon instant minced onion__
   (or chop about 1 tablespoon of fresh)
salt and pepper, to taste

Combine and
have all ready
and chilled,
if in a forehanded
mood.

__leaf lettuce__, well washed and dried, placed on bottom half
      of roll, then generously heaped with the
      filling and top of roll pushed down on all.

You may substitute ham for the bologna and sliced bread
for rolls.

## Merelyn Reeve's __Favorite Open Sandwich__

You may gild this
lily with cooked bacon
topping if the mood dictates.

A slice of __pumpernickel or dark rye bread__, spread with
__mayonnaise__, then some
__raw spinach or sprouts__ and
__sliced tomato__ carefully covering the greens and
__sliced sweet onion__ spread over the tomato and some
__sharp Cheddar cheese__ covering all.      No salt.

All this prepared on foil, so there's no mess and its
ready to slide under broiler until cheese melts.
        YUM

# Broiled Reuben Sandwiches (for 6)

12 slices dark rye or pumpernickel bread
butter the bread and place on foil-lined
    cookie sheet, butter side down.

½ cup mayonnaise, mixed with some
chili sauce in amount you prefer.
          To this add:

pimiento
green pepper } chopped very fine.
celery     Optional but savory.
        Salt, a shake

} Spread this mixture on 6 of the bread slices.

12 slices corned beef
6 slices Swiss cheese
sauerkraut (16 ounces)

} For each sandwich, place on the mayonnaise mixture one slice of corned beef and one slice of cheese. Then spread on the sauerkraut and then another slice of corned beef. Top with the other slice of bread, butter side out!

Toast under broiler on both sides. There are those who fry Reubens on a griddle, and do so if you prefer. I happen to like this method better. It's also better for you and there's no griddle to clean up.

Here's a good standby:

## Olive-Nut Spread

6 ounces cream cheese, softened
⅓ cup mayonnaise
½ cup chopped pecans
1 cup chopped pimiento-stuffed olives
2 tablespoons olive juice
pepper, to taste — no salt

} Mix thoroughly. Refrigerate before spreading on bread. This can make hearty sandwiches or the daintiest, tiny tea sandwiches.

# Hot Turkey or Chicken Sandwiches (Serves 6)

3 tablespoons butter, melted over hot water in top of double boiler.

3 tablespoons flour

¾ teaspoon salt

pepper, to taste

1 teaspoon prepared mustard
} Mix into above butter.

Remove from heat and stir in very slowly

2 cups milk ↶ Return to heat and stir constantly until thick and smooth.

1½ cups grated American "rat trap" cheese (sharp Cheddar),
     stirred into white sauce until melted.

6 slices toast, placed in buttered, shallow baking dish.

Turkey or chicken, either diced or in slices, arranged on toast.

Pour the cheese sauce carefully over all and sprinkle with paprika.
Place in preheated 450° oven for 10 minutes.
                    Have ready:

Slices of tomato
Cooked bacon
} as topping for the hot sandwiches.

Great luncheon or supper dish.
If you make this just once it won't be for the last time.

## Soup

# About Soup — Soothing Soup

" Beautiful soup! Who cares for fish, game or any other dish? Who would not give all else for two pennyworth only of beautiful soup?"

Lewis Carroll

A few years ago I had the pleasure of taking one of Julie Dannenbaum's famous cooking courses at The Greenbrier in White Sulphur Springs. Among the experts attending were a few humble housewives like myself, who just plain liked to cook. There was one woman in the group a bit humbler than the rest and for good reason. When a discussion took place as to what, in particular, each person was anxious to learn, this neophyte spoke up and said, "I've always wanted to know how to make soup du jour." ! To say this remark brought down the house is an understatement.

When talking of soup, I mean hot soup, both winter and summer. (Although I've included a few, very few, cold ones.) New cookbooks abound with ice-cold concoctions, from vichyssoise, which started the chilly trend, to gazpacho and even fruit soups which make me think I'm eating dessert first. Fine for those who like them and have bovine digestions, but there's nothing like hot soup to pave the way for the good food and wine that may follow.

In this maidless age one is inclined to skip the soup course altogether, the switching of plates proving a lot of work, and soup constituting too much to consume anyway. Soup is more often a main luncheon dish today, along with salad and/or a sandwich. However, a clear broth or consommé, hot, mostly calorieless, is a merciful way to treat the inner man after cold cocktails and before the main course. So here's a modern compromise: Have an urn, tureen, double boiler, or even the soup kettle itself (you can wrap a pretty napkin or towel around it) appear on your bar set-up surrounded by cups and let guests help themselves. It is amazing to see how enthusiastically they switch from the cocktail hour to the soup course and how warmed and ready they are for your carefully planned meal.

Hot broth is always popular at a brunch or tea. In fact, serving just broth and Melba toast (plain or herbed (page 27 ) at a small tea makes a hit with those who are watching calories. And who isn't?

Equipment for soup making consists of just three basics: a stock pot, some sort of strainer, and a piece of cheesecloth. An enamel ware or stainless steel pot is best. So is long, slow cooking. (I'm talking about the broth or stock that is the basis of many varieties of soup, as well as a fine potion to drink on its own.) When the broth is sufficiently cooked, place a large colander or strainer over any receptacle large enough to hold all the liquid, and line it with a piece of cheesecloth. Don't try to pour all at once. By that route lies splashing and burns. Spoon out most of the "glup" into the cheesecloth-lined strainer. Then you can safely pour the last of the liquid. When all is sufficiently cooled and the big bones discarded, it is easy to twist the cheesecloth so as to squeeze out the last bit of goodness. Cover the broth and chill overnight. More about that in a minute. As you wash up the cooking utensils, wash out the cheesecloth. I've had a piece of cheesecloth that has lasted for years. It's large enough so I can double it to do a thorough straining job and come up with a passably clear broth. I don't bother to clarify the broth any further. If you are a zealot and want to clarify, get out The Joy of Cooking and read their perfect directions for so doing.

Chilling broth overnight is imperative so as to remove the last vestige of fat. A true story about Enrico Caruso underscores my paranoia on the subject. Caruso served in the artillery in Italy in his youth and, of course, was given to singing as he went about his duties. One day he did not sing at all, an event so unusual that the major sent for him to ask him what was wrong. Caruso said, "I cannot sing on greasy soup." The story ended happily in that excellent and greaseless soup was served from then on. If soup is well chilled, it is so easy to remove the fat that rises to the top. Greasy soup is a no-no aesthetically, taste wise, health wise.

Never throw away a bone from any type of meat! It's not only wasteful but stupid, for bones are what give soup its gelatinous goodness and build the bones of those who partake of it.

Likewise pan drippings. It's hard not to shed tears when I've seen someone take a nice, crusty roasting pan, squirt some detergent and hot water into it and leave it to soak. Put some water in the pan, yes. Then simmer on stove and stir and scrape to loosen every bit of the lovely browned juices, pour into a dish and refrigerate until needed. The delicious, gelatinous material that forms beneath its covering of fat has more authority than any bouillon cube you can buy. Put it in soup, spread it on a meat sandwich, turn it into a succulent sauce.

Doctors who, at long last, are taking some nutrition courses in medical school I believe will bear me out when I say that hot soups are even more necessary in summer than in winter. They help to offset all the icy food and drink we pour into our systems in the heat of summer. American refrigerators are wonders of the world in one way, but they have also contributed to making us the most ulcer - prone people on earth. So here follow some tangible blessings with which to start a meal, some "soups du jour," mostly hot, always greaseless, and let's hope they'll make you sing.

Julie Dannenbaum's          Brown Stock (This makes 2 or 3 quarts)

2 pounds lean beef, brisket or shin, cubed
2 pounds beef bones
1 veal knuckle (if you can get it)
2 carrots, washed and sliced
2 onions, skins on — 2 cloves stuck in each
2 celery ribs, leaves and all, sliced

Put all this in a buttered baking pan and place in preheated 450° oven for ½ to 1 hour. Keep stirring it around. When nice and brown, pour off grease, and transfer to stock pot.

Put some water in the roasting pan and scrape up all the brown goodness and pour into stock pot along with:

4 quarts water (cold)
1 cup dry white wine
1 tomato, cut up
1 tablespoon salt
½ teaspoon pepper
1 clove garlic, mashed
½ teaspoon thyme
1 bay leaf
3 sprigs parsley

Bring all this to a boil and skim! Simmer at least 4 hours, half covered, and keep skimming as needed.

When sufficiently cooked remove from heat and allow to cool somewhat before trying to handle. With a slotted spoon remove bones and vegetables from broth and then pour the broth into a colander (lined with cheesecloth) resting on a clean vessel. Chill the strained broth quickly. (You may want to freeze some in small containers.) You now have pure gold on hand, to serve as is as a delicious broth, or as the basis of elegant soups, stews and sauces. There are no canned products that can approach this, though as time and energy savers we are often grateful for them.

# Chicken Stock or Broth (The way I make it.)
(Makes 2 plus quarts.)

4 or 5 pounds chicken backs and necks, well washed and placed in stock pot with the following:

3 quarts cold water
2 carrots, sliced, skin on
2 onions, sliced, skin on
4 ribs of celery with their leaves
3 sprigs parsley
½ teaspoon thyme
6 peppercorns
2 cloves ⎤
½ bay leaf ⎬ These are optional and used if you like your broth with more seasoning.
½ teaspoon allspice ⎦
2 teaspoons salt added at last of cooking

Simmer all this for 4 hours or more, half covered. Skim and strain exactly as directed for Brown Stock on previous page.

Have your butcher let you know when chicken backs and necks are available. They cost very little and make excellent stock.

If you need chicken meat for salad, sandwiches, etc., stew a whole 4 or 5 pound bird, or cut up chicken, and make your stock that way. But as soon as the meat is tender, remove and cool it. Cut off the needed meat and return all bones and skin to the cook pot and proceed with the long simmering, as above.

Excellent stocks are made from the carcass of roast chicken or any leftover chicken bones. Season and simmer as above, including any gravy, pan drippings and cooked vegetables you don't know what to do with.

Always remove all fat from the top of chilled stocks before using. But as fat makes an airtight seal, leave it in place until ready to use.

# Effortless Avocado Soup  (serves 4)

1 ripe avocado, peeled, pitted
2 cups chicken broth
2 tablespoons white wine
½ teaspoon curry
½ teaspoon salt
pepper, freshly ground
1 cup light cream

Blend in blender.

Serve hot (but do not boil) or cold.

~~~~~~~~~~~~~~~~

Soup Hint:
　　　Put some chopped fresh spinach or lettuce in the bottom of each bowl or cup. Then ladle hot, clear broth over it. A green, nourishing, tasty touch.

~~~~~~~~~~~~~~~~

Weezie's　　　California Consommé

In soup bowls or cups place several dainty slices of avocados and a thin slice or two of lemon. Pour boiling hot chicken broth over all. Add 1 tablespoon (or less) of sherry. Serve at once. Delicious and different. Good luncheon dish with salad and dessert.

~~~~~~~~~~~~~~~~

# Pinto Bean Soup   or   The Herb Buff's Delight
### (Serves 8 to 10)

2 cups pinto beans, washed and soaked in large soup kettle overnight. Have sufficient water to cover beans. Drain the next morning.

1 pound slice of ham (or less), trimmed of fat and cubed
1 quart water
22 ounce can tomato juice
1 quart chicken stock
3 cloves garlic, minced
3 tablespoons parsley, chopped
1/4 cup chopped green pepper
3 tablespoons brown sugar
1 tablespoon chili powder
1 teaspoon crushed bay leaves
1 teaspoon oregano
1/2 teaspoon ground cumin
1/2 teaspoon crushed rosemary
1/2 teaspoon celery seed
1/2 teaspoon thyme
1/2 teaspoon marjoram
1/2 teaspoon basil
1/4 teaspoon curry
4 whole cloves

Add all this to soaked and drained beans.

Simmer gently, covered, until beans are very tender (4 hours, more or less). Salt to taste.

Serve in soup bowls.

A tablespoon or more of sherry may be added to each bowl of soup if desired. A nice touch is to serve the sherry in a cruet or small pitcher to allow individual choice.

Serve this tasty, hearty soup with crusty bread or rolls.

Soup freezes well.

## Bon Mélange  (serves 8 or more)

**3 cups dried beans, split peas, and barley**

Wash thoroughly and place in stewing kettle.
Use any and every type of bean that appeals
to you, with some peas and barley to fill out
the 3 cups. (You may use just dried beans if
more convenient. Then you have Bean Soup
rather than Bon Mélange. You can't lose
either way.) Pour over this:

**3 quarts water** along with

**2 ½ teaspoons salt**

**¼ teaspoon thyme** ⎫
**1 teaspoon parsley** ⎬ dried. Use more
                          if fresh.

**½ bay leaf** ⎭

**ham hock or ham bone** – if lacking both, I've used
small slice of ham trimmed of
fat, or a chunk of Canadian bacon.

⎱ Simmer, covered, for 3 hours.

**1 can tomatoes** (16 ounces or more)

**2 cups chopped onion**

**2 cups chopped celery**

**2 cloves garlic, minced**

**1 teaspoon chili powder**

**juice of ½ lemon**

Add this to above after it
has cooked the 3 hours.
Now simmer uncovered for about
another 1 ½ hours.
Check for need of salt and pepper.

Remove the ham hock or bone or whatever and the bay leaf if you
can find it. Cut up any clear pieces of ham and return to soup. Lacking
ham meat, cut up 2 or 3 hot dogs into thin slices and add toward end
of cooking. Chill and forget the soup for a day or so. It
improves with age.  A wonderful winter meal served with
crusty French bread.

# Carrot Soup (about 8 cups)

<u>2 tablespoons butter</u>, melted in pot large enough for whole recipe.

<u>2 good-sized onions</u>, cut up and added to butter. Stir around for 2 or 3 minutes.

<u>4 generous carrots</u>, cut up

<u>1 stalk celery</u>, scraped and cut up.
(The scraping removes the strings that even a blender fails to disintegrate thoroughly.)

<u>1 generous potato</u>, peeled and cut up.

<u>1 parsnip</u>, optional, cut up

<u>1 white turnip</u>, optional, cut up

<u>1 quart of chicken broth</u>

Add to onions. Cover pan and bring to boil. Let simmer for about 30 minutes or until vegetables are tender but not mushy. Blend in blender. Return to original kettle. Then add:

<u>1 small can (5 ounces) evaporated milk</u>
(or <u>1 cup real cream</u>)

<u>Salt and pepper</u>, to taste

<u>nutmeg</u>, just a slight grating, but not so as to notice it.

Heat to serve but <u>do not boil</u>. I like it with my own homemade croutons.
Can be served <u>chilled</u> with a dollop of yogurt.

This soup is equally acceptable as party fare or a soothing reviver for anyone "feeling poorly."

# Cream of Cauliflower Soup (serves 4)

1 medium cauliflower, separated into flowerets and
boiled in

2 cups chicken broth until barely tender, no more.
Put into blender with the following:

one 10¾ ounce can Cream of Chicken Soup  ⎫
½ teaspoon lemon juice                    ⎬ Blend
⅛ teaspoon nutmeg                         ⎭

salt and pepper if your taste buds indicate, added after blending.

Heat and serve.

(This recipe is also good substituting string beans or broccoli
for cauliflower.)

~~~~~~~~~~

There's no better way of getting plenty of
health-giving vegetables into the diet than by making
them into puréed soups. Blenders and food processors
have turned that chore into a cinch.

~~~~~~~~~~

# Super Celery Soup (serves 4)

2 cups chicken broth, your own, canned or made with bouillon cubes*

2 cups roughly cut-up celery

1 cut-up onion

Combine and simmer until vegetables are only slightly cooked. Blend in blender and strain back into same soup pot and add:

1 cup evaporated milk (or light cream)

salt
pepper
celery seed } to taste

This is now ready to heat for serving. Do not boil. As soup is heating add:

1 cup celery, finely chopped (to give crunch and added flavor).
Garnish with a touch of chopped celery leaves.
Serve with croutons, plain or herbed. (page 218)

The best soup I ever made was with the pan juices from a roast turkey breast instead of chicken broth.

* Knorr-Swiss is my favorite brand. Be careful — one cube makes 2 cups of broth, unlike other brands that only make 1 cup.

# Petey Foster's <u>Cheddar Cheese Soup</u> (serves 8)

<u>¼ cup butter</u> (½ stick), heated in kettle of size to hold all.
To the hot butter add:

<u>½ cup finely chopped onion</u>
<u>½ cup finely chopped carrots</u>  } Sauté until slightly softened.
<u>½ cup finely chopped celery</u>  } Then stir in carefully:

<u>1½ tablespoons cornstarch</u>  } Mixed. When this is well stirred
<u>¼ cup flour</u> - - - - - - - }  into above, remove from heat and
 gradually stir in:

<u>1 quart chicken broth</u> - - - - } Return to <u>low</u> heat and stir
<u>1 quart half and half cream</u> } religiously until smooth and
 } thickened . Then add:

<u>½ teaspoon soda</u>  and

<u>2½ cups sharp grated Cheddar cheese</u>, tightly packed.
 Cook and stir only until cheese
 melts. Then add:
<u>salt</u> and <u>pepper</u>, to taste, and serve garnished with
<u>chopped parsley</u>, plenty of it.

(If you delay serving soup, its best to reheat in double boiler to
avoid scorching, which happens all too easily.)

Petey serves this to hungry mobs
of family and friends who gather
annually at Christmas Cove in
Maine. Its nearly a whole meal in
itself and devastatingly delicious.

Judy's     Cucumber Borsch    (Serves 6)

<u>2 medium cucumbers</u>, peeled, cut in half the long way,
seeds dug out with spoon.

<u>1 pound cooked beets</u>, canned or fresh

<u>½ a small onion</u>

<u>1 small rib celery</u>, chopped fine
(so there'll be no strings in soup*)

<u>sprigs of parsley</u> (a few, stems removed)

} Blend in blender with enough of the broth below to liquify sufficiently.

<u>6 cups chicken broth</u> made with Knorr-Swiss bouillon cubes.

Heat what is left of this broth after the blending process and combine with above.

<u>pepper</u>, to taste

<u>salt</u> probably not necessary. You decide.

If you want cold borsch, chill without further heating. If hot, bring up to boil and serve at once. In either case garnish with

<u>sour cream</u>, sprinkled with plenty of <u>dill weed</u> (dried or fresh)

* For some reason even a blender does not get rid of all the stringy part of celery. You can scrape it off, but it is time consuming.

# New England Golden Fish Chowder (serves 6 to 8)

3 tablespoons butter, melted in large saucepan

1 onion, chopped
1 rib celery, chopped } sauté in the butter until softened.

3 tablespoons flour, stirred into above and stirred and cooked a bit. Then remove from heat.

5 cups milk, poured slowly and stirred constantly into above flour mixture. Return to fire and, on low heat and stirring often, bring to simmer. Do not boil! Careful not to scorch.

2 cups diced potatoes, boiled in a cup or more of water for 5 minutes, in separate pan.

1 pound fish fillets (cut into bite-sized pieces). I like flounder but you may use whatever fish you prefer. Add fish to partially cooked potatoes along with:

1 teaspoon salt and more water
¼ teaspoon pepper          Simmer for 10 to
1 bay leaf                 15 minutes, until
¼ teaspoon thyme           potatoes and fish are
¼ teaspoon dill            cooked. Then add all
                           to the heated milk
                           with

2 cups (8 ounces) shredded Cheddar cheese. When cheese has melted, the chowder is ready to serve with split, buttered, toasted "common crackers" (variously called Vermont crackers, chowder crackers, Cross Crackers).

(Fish out the bay leaf.)

# Lettuce Soup (serves 4 to 6)

1 onion, chopped
1 stalk celery, generous, chopped } simmer in:
2 tablespoons butter until slightly softened, using saucepan
large enough for whole recipe. Then add:

2 tablespoons flour and stir well for about 3 minutes. Remove from
fire and pour on while stirring constantly:

4 cups chicken broth that has been heated. Stir well until lump-free
and add:

6 cups packed, shredded lettuce ~ Boston lettuce recommended —
(about 2 heads) or any garden
lettuce except iceberg. Simmer
and stir a good 5 minutes. Then add:

½ cup packed watercress leaves (optional but fine addition), cooking
them only 1 minute. Season with:

¼ teaspoon dried tarragon (or more of chopped fresh tarragon)

salt and pepper, to taste
Blend all this in blender (probably necessitating
2 loads) to a coarse purée. It is now ready to heat or chill.

A great soup at any time, but especially
when lettuce abounds in the summer garden.

# Cream of Mushroom Soup  (Serves 4 plus)

4 tablespoons butter, melted in saucepan

1 onion
½ pound mushrooms, stems and all
1 rib celery
some parsley (about 1 tablespoon when chopped)

} Chop all this roughly, then sauté in above butter for about 15 minutes.

3 cups chicken broth
1 heaping tablespoon flour

} Blend together in blender. Then pour over the sautéed vegetables. Stir and heat until slightly thickened. Return to blender and blend very little. You want a textured soup. Transfer soup to top of double boiler and add:

1 cup light cream
(or you may substitute evaporated milk)
¼ cup sherry
Salt and pepper, to taste

} When ready to serve, bring up to heat over boiling water and serve at once, garnished with

chopped chives, fresh or dried

You will find this soup a happy contrast to the ubiquitous canned variety.

# Parsley Soup    (serves 4)

2 potatoes, cut up
2 onions, cut up
generous dab of butter
very little water
}  Simmer until vegetables are cooked. Do not drain. Transfer to blender.

1 bunch parsley, well washed, stems removed.
1 can chicken broth (10¾ ounces)
        or equivalent of home made
salt and pepper, to taste
curry powder, a pinch
Worcestershire sauce, a dash
}  Add this to the vegetables in blender. Blend well.

2 cups milk (or half milk, half cream
  — or you may substitute evaporated milk for cream.)
}  Pour this into a double boiler. Then stir in the contents of the blender. Check the seasoning.

When ready to serve, bring up to heat over boiling water. Serve with croutons.

    This is my favorite soup. In the spring of the year you may substitute tender dandelion greens for parsley! Delicious, nutritious.
    Parsley is sometimes fed to race horses to give them added energy. Why not you?

# Parsnip Soup (serves 4 to 6)

As served at the St. Johnsbury House in St. Johnsbury, Vermont, in the days of its former glory.

1 good-sized onion, chopped and sautéed lightly in
3 tablespoons butter, in kettle large enough to hold all of recipe.
                              Then add:

1 cup water
2 potatoes, peeled and sliced
3 large parsnips, scraped and sliced
} Cover and cook until vegetables are just tender. Then transfer to blender and blend along with

2 cups whole milk
2 tablespoons flour
} When all is blended, return to cooking kettle and add

2 cups more of milk
1 teaspoon salt
pepper, freshly ground, to taste
} Heat slowly while stirring often, until a bit more thickened. Try to keep below boiling point. Serve at once or hold and heat later being careful not to scorch. A double boiler is safest.

Garnish with paprika or parsley or chives.
Serve with croutons (page 218).

# Parsnip Bisque (Serves 4)

2 tablespoons butter⎫ Heated in saucepan large enough
1 tablespoon oil   ⎬ to hold all that follows.

1 leek, white part only, chopped⎫ Sauté in above hot fat
   (Lacking leeks, chop 1 onion.)⎬ for about 3 minutes, stirring.
3 parsnips, scraped, diced ⎭

1 tablespoon flour      ⎫ Sprinkle
1 teaspoon brown sugar⎬ over above
                       ⎭ vegetables and stir well.

3 cups beef bouillon, added gradually to above, stirring well.
         Bring to boil, then down to simmer. Cover and
         cook until parsnips are tender, which only
         takes a short time. Then blend all in blender
         and return to saucepan.
         When ready to serve, add:

1 cup milk or light cream — Reheat but do not boil.
         Season to taste with
salt and pepper and garnish generously with
chopped parsley

~~~~~~~~~~~~~~~~

         The parsnip, first cousin to the carrot, is native to Eurasia
and, since the times of the Greeks and Romans, has been an important food staple.
Then along came the potato, after the age of discovery, which caused this fine
vegetable to take a back seat. Try moving it up front. Its flavor is unique.
(See vegetable section of this book.)

~~~~~~~~~~~~~~~~

# Super Pea Soup (serves 6 to 8)

2 ten-ounce packages of frozen peas
2 cups shredded iceberg lettuce
(any variety is permissible)
2 cups chicken broth

} Place in saucepan.
Simmer 10 minutes only.
Transfer to blender.

½ teaspoon curry
Salt and pepper, to taste
2 tablespoons butter

} Added to above in blender.
Blend well. Return to saucepan
and hold until ready to serve.

2 cups light cream, added to above at serving time.
Heat but do not boil — and serve.
Or chill thoroughly, if you prefer, for
hot weather fare.

chopped mint is the perfect garnish.

Being particularly fond
of this soup, I make it
often to gorge on alone,
Halving the recipe and
sometimes using one small
can of evaporated milk
in place of cream. Lacking
fresh mint, the dried, bottled
variety, crumbled, does
very well as embellishment.

# Phyllis's Pumpkin Soup (Serves 8)

¼ cup butter (½ stick), melted in pan large enough for whole recipe.

1 large white onion, sliced ⎤ Cook this until slightly
¾ cup sliced scallions (white part only) ⎦ browned in above butter.

2 sixteen-ounce cans pumpkin
4 cups chicken broth
1 bay leaf
½ teaspoon sugar
½ teaspoon curry powder
¼ teaspoon nutmeg
parsley — a few sprigs
2 cups rich milk
salt ⎤ to taste
pepper, freshly ground ⎦

Add all this to above onions. Mix well. Simmer oh so gently but do not boil — for 45 minutes. Strain, reheat (or chill if you desire cold soup). Serve garnished with :

yogurt or sour cream or whipped cream
paprika, a touch
parsley, a sprig

Pumpkin is imperative for Thanksgiving. Why not have it in the form of soup first rather than pie last?

# Spinach Soup (Serves 4)

Spinach, about 10 ounces fresh from garden ⎫ Cook together in about
　　　　or a 10-ounce bag from grocery ⎬ 1 cup water until just
　　　　or a 10-ounce frozen package ⎪ wilted, no more (about
1 medium onion, cut up _ _ _ _ _ ⎭ 5 minutes). Do not drain.

Transfer to blender and add:

One 10¾ ounce can of chicken broth

(You may substitute Campbell's Consommé 　Blend and return to original
　for a change.) 　　　　　　　　　　Cook pot. Add:

1 tablespoon lemon juice ⎫
a slight grating of nutmeg ⎪ Heat and serve or chill
salt and pepper, to taste ⎬ and serve.
1 tablespoon butter ⎭ Garnish with hard-boiled egg,
　　　　　　　　　　　　finely chopped (I use a potato
ricer), or sour cream or sweet cream or yogurt.
Good served with Melba toast or herbed croutons (page 218).

A bright green nourishing delight served hot or cold.

Watercress Soup: You may substitute 2 bunches of
　　　　　　　　watercress for the spinach, but don't precook
　　　　　　　　watercress, just the onion.
Sorrel Soup: Substitute 10 ounces of sorrel for spinach. Don't
　　　　　　precook it, just the onion. And skip the lemon.
　　　　　　Sorrel is "first cousin to 'sour grass.'"

Above soups may become cream soups by addition of a cup of cream
added at the last. (Heat but do not boil.) For creamier consistency add
1 tablespoon flour when doing blending process. I find the soups sufficiently
delicious without the added calories of cream and flour, though they do enhance.

# Old Fashioned Cream of Tomato Soup (serves 4 to 6)

This used to be served at my grandmother's home in a tureen and for a first course. Lots more food followed. But we walked miles in those days, and New England winters were cold and hunger inducing. How I loved this soup! It was always served with croutons (page 218).

1 quart of milk, scalded slowly with
1 onion, stuck with several cloves, and
½ bay leaf

> Don't hurry this. You want to draw out the flavor.

2 cups cut-up tomatoes, fresh or canned
½ cup chopped celery
1 small onion, cut up
2 teaspoons sugar

> Simmer, covered, for around 15 minutes. When cooked add ¼ teaspoon soda (an ancient custom but a good one in this case).

4 tablespoons butter, heated in saucepan of size to hold whole recipe.
4 tablespoons flour, stirred into butter and cooked about 5 minutes. Remove from heat and slowly stir in the scalded milk from which you've removed the onion and bay leaf. Return to heat and stir well until slightly thickened! Now strain the foamy tomato mixture into this white sauce. Stir, heat, but do not boil.

salt and pepper, to taste.                    Don't forget the croutons.

This recipe may be done ahead and reheated in double boiler.

Canned soup cannot compete with this. Serve at a winter luncheon or Sunday supper along with some dainty open sandwiches. Guests will bless you.

# Garden Tomato Soup (Serves 6 to 8)

(As served at Woodbine Cottage in Sunapee Harbor, New Hampshire.
Thanks to Dorothy Bryant.)

8 pounds tomatoes (about 1 dozen big ones)
(or use 4 *2½ cans of tomatoes)
2 ribs celery with leaves
5 cloves
1 bay leaf
1 sprig parsley

Bring to boil and then simmer gently for 2 hours, covered. Tomatoes should be cut up roughly, skin and all. When cooked — strain.

4 tablespoons butter, heated in saucepan of size for whole recipe.
4 tablespoons flour, cooked and stirred in butter a few minutes.

Remove from heat and slowly stir in the strained tomato liquid.

Salt — around 3 teaspoons if fresh tomatoes used.
Less salt for canned tomatoes.
3 tablespoons sugar

Add to above. Return to heat. Bring just to boil, stirring diligently.

You may serve this tomato essence with a
dash of ground cloves
a dollop of whipped cream
a sprinkle of chopped basil

This soup served with a toasted cheese sandwich makes a meal for the gods.

* A *2½ can is almost a quart and varies from 28 to 30 ounces.

# Turkey Chowder (Serves 12)
### (By Marjorie Oxford of Shreveport, Louisiana)
#### All in one pot from start to finish!

½ cup (¼ pound) butter, heated in adequate-sized kettle.
4 onions, coarsely chopped, and cooked until softened in the butter.

4 medium potatoes, peeled, cubed or sliced
4 teaspoons salt
½ teaspoon pepper
2 cups water
1 chicken bouillon cube (or substitute 2 cups chicken or turkey stock)

> Add to above and simmer, covered, until potatoes are tender.

6 cups milk
1 cup light cream
1 can (16.1 oz.) cream-style corn
2 cans (15.5 oz.) whole kernel corn
4 cups cooked turkey, cut to bite size
¼ teaspoon thyme
1½ teaspoons paprika

> Add all this to above. Bring up to heat gradually. (Milk scorches easily.) Do not boil!

3 ribs celery, chopped fine
6 scallions, chopped fine
parsley (a modest handful), chopped
2 tablespoons butter (optional)

> Stir in at last minute for crunchy perfection, and serve!

A good idea is to have roast turkey breast (page 88) for dinner one evening, then you'll have the makings for this fabulous chowder any time thereafter.

# Spring Vegetable Soup (serves 6)

2 tablespoons butter, heated in saucepan large enough for the whole recipe.

1 small onion, chopped
1 leek (white part only), well washed, chopped
    (Lacking a leek, use 2 onions)
1 clove garlic, minced

} Sauté in the hot butter until soft. Then add to this all of the following:

1 quart chicken broth (your own, canned or bouillon cubes)

1 potato
1 small zucchini
1 cup spinach     } chopped
1 cup lettuce
1 tomato, peeled

salt and pepper, to taste

Bring all up to simmer and cook slowly for ½ hour or more.
Serve with side dishes of:
grated Parmesan cheese
chopped parsley

Spring Vegetable Soup calls for a crusty loaf of French or Italian bread as accompaniment.

# Cream of Zucchini Soup (2 generous servings, 4 dainty)

2 cups boiling water, in which dissolve
3 chicken bouillon cubes (Be careful if you use Knorr-Swiss which comes in 2-cup size. 1½ cubes of it sufficient.)

1 medium onion, cut up
2 heaping cups young zucchini, about, cut up

Add this to above and cook until crisp-tender, no more. Then blend in blender and return to cooking pot. Then add:

1 small can evaporated milk
pepper, to taste

Stir all together. Heat when ready to serve, but do not boil.

Garnish with a dab of sour cream, or chopped parsley, or croutons.

This is as simple as rolling off a log, but in its simplicity lies its charm.

For a more highly seasoned zucchini soup, see next page.

## Bess Shaver's <u>Zucchini Soup</u>
(Makes about 8 servings of 1 cup each. Serve hot or cold.)

<u>4 slices of bacon</u>, coarsely chopped and cooked to crispness in kettle large enough to contain whole recipe. Remove cooked bacon bits to paper towel. Drain off fat, leaving <u>1 tablespoon</u> in kettle.

<u>1 large onion</u>, chopped
<u>1 clove garlic</u>, chopped } Brown slightly in the 1 tablespoon of fat.

<u>1 can (10½ ounce) Campbell's Consommé</u>

<u>2½ cups water</u>

<u>1 teaspoon salt</u>

<u>¼ cup chopped fresh parsley</u> (or 1 heaping tablespoon of dried parsley)

<u>1 tablespoon chopped fresh basil</u> (or 1 teaspoon dried)

<u>freshly ground pepper</u> — a good sprinkling

<u>6 (about) moderate-sized zucchini</u>, sliced

Toss all this into kettle above. Bring to a simmer and cook until zucchini is just barely tender. Then blend in blender. Serve very hot or very cold, garnished with

the reserved <u>bacon</u> above and grated <u>Parmesan cheese</u>.

# Bird — Beast — Fish

About Bird and Beast and Fish, 72

From *The Legend of Sleepy Hollow* by Washington Irving

Ichabod Crane, as the schoolteacher of Sleepy Hollow, spends his week of "boarding 'round" at the home of the wealthiest farmer of the area, one Baltus Van Tassel.

"The pedagogue's (Ichabod's) mouth watered as he looked upon this sumptuous promise of luxurious winter fare. In his devouring mind's eye, he pictured to himself every roasting pig running about, with a pudding in its belly and an apple in its mouth; the pigeons were snugly put to bed in a comfortable pie and tucked in with a coverlet of crust; the geese were swimming in their own gravy; and the ducks pairing cosily in dishes, like snug married couples, with a decent competency of onion sauce.* In the porkers he saw carved out the future sleek side of bacon and juicy relishing ham; not a turkey, but he beheld daintily trussed up with its gizzard under its wing, and, peradventure, a necklace of savory sausages; and even bright chanticleer himself lay sprawling on his back, in a side dish, with uplifted claws, as if craving that quarter which his chivalrous spirit disdained to ask while living.

"As the enraptured Ichabod fancied all this, and as he rolled his great green eyes over the fat meadow lands, the rich fields of wheat, of rye, of buckwheat, and Indian corn, and the orchards burdened with ruddy fruit, which surrounded the warm tenement of Van Tassel, his heart yearned after the damsel who was to inherit these domains."

Although a modern supermarket is hardly the bucolic scene that gladdened the heart of Ichabod Crane, I believe his

* Onion Sauce ~ see page 268

"great green eyes" would pop right out of his head could he behold the miraculous displays of foods that we take so much for granted. Supermarkets of today make available a wealth of produce that Ichabod could not have imagined in his wildest dreams.

It has been stated that the secret of spreading a fine table is to be a conscientious shopper. Shop often so things are fresh. We hear so much about the long-lived Georgians of Russia, whose secret of longevity seems to be due, in part, to the fact that they throw any leftovers to the dogs and start fresh at each meal! This is an extremity not to be recommended, but a kernel of suggestion lies therein.

When there are meat specials at the market, its the time to buy for freezing. Remember that quick freezing and careful wrapping are two essentials. Beef, lamb and veal can be kept frozen for up to a year, but pork, poultry and fish should be limited to a few months. Strangely enough, cured meats, like ham, turn rancid fairly quickly due to the salt.

In the United States, with 1/15th of the world's population, we eat 1/3rd of the world's meat. Since the early 1970's we've eaten less red meat whereas our use of poultry has tripled. "The competitive battle will heat up," predicts Joseph Doyle, an analyst from Smith Barney, Harris Upham and Company. "It's a growing category. The American consumer has shifted toward chicken." Praises be to chicken that is not only inexpensive but one of the meats doctors recommend. And everyone seems to love it, unlike fish. It is one of the safer things to serve from a variety of standpoints. So hooray for the "Little Red Hen". You will find lots of recipes here in the chicken category, many prepared in easy stove-to-table cookware that even Tiffany's is selling these days. (I lean toward Corning ware.) Be a collector of such baking dishes. They are great work savers.

Like cheese and wine, beef is improved with aging. Flavor develops as does tenderness. (Be sure to make friends with a butcher who can guide you in such matters.) When I was a child, my grandfather used to take me to Faneuil Hall market in Boston, where his butcher had steaks and roasts hanging for his inspection. There had to be just the right amount of mould thereon to pass examination. It looked awful to me, but what beef it was when served!

Searing meat (according to the expert, Harold McGee) has nothing to do with nutrition or juiciness, only with taste. Seared meats are tastier. (Seems to me I've always known that from experience, but he speaks from scientific investigation.) Of course, if meat is grossly overdone it may detract from the nutritional value. But McGee comforts me by stating that one may recoup the fluid losses of overcooked meat by making gravy from the drippings, which I do, or save every scrap of the good drippings for later use. I'm not guilty of overcooking beef, I believe, but slippery chicken and pink pork and underdone lamb are anathema to me, so I err on the side of long cooking and like it.

A doctor friend, who should know, assures me that pork may be even more acceptable than beef (from a health standpoint) because pigs are no longer fattened as intensively as they used to be. Marbled rare beef can put more fat into the system than well cooked pork.

When it comes to carving any sort of roast — beef, lamb, poultry, ham, to name a few — always let it rest about 15 minutes before cutting. For one thing, it continues to cook after removal from the oven; for another, it is easier to carve after that rest period. And have a sharp carving knife! Sawing away at meat with a dull knife squeezes out precious juices and makes the meat drier, not to mention frustrating the carver. Have well-warmed dinner plates.

Meats such as liver, low in connective tissue, should be cooked very little, as long cooking toughens them. Hearts and gizzards, on the contrary, are muscular meat and should be cooked long and slowly.

Now about fish and shellfish:
They fall into a special meat category due to different muscle organization. They should be cooked as little as possible, long cooking making them dry and tough. (I've learned this the hard way, so take it not only from the experts but from a sadder and wiser housewife.)

The reason there's a dearth of fish recipes in this book is because, I regret to say, I don't like some fish and it's difficult to write with enthusiasm about something that turns me off. Shellfish I adore, likewise caviar, and good old New England Fish Cakes (page 114, Bentley Farm Cookbook) and tuna fish.

There's no rhyme or reason to my strange likes and prejudices. Yes, there is some reason and this is it:

As a child we had fish every Friday due to the religious scruples of the help. It was the day of the week I dreaded, for my stepmother was of the clean - your - plate - or - else school. We usually had boiled halibut, the loathsome odor of which greeted us as we came in the door from school, my brothers and sisters and I.

One fateful Friday I went through the usual routine of pretending to eat the fish, until my stepmother's attention was focused on one of my siblings. Then came the sleight-of-hand act of slipping the fish under the dining room table onto a convenient ledge that projected out from the top of the table leg next to which I sat. What was my horror when I saw the family cat, which usually dwelt in the kitchen, making a beeline for my hidden halibut. Pretending the cat had scratched me I grabbed him and racing from the table, threw him out the front door with more strength and skill than I knew I possessed. The poor cat made a perfect arc through the air.

By some miracle the long white tablecloth that always graced the table at mealtime shielded the scattered fish from view and I was able, later, to remove the evidence before discovery. So, many types of fish remain abhorrent to me, increased, no doubt by memories such as this.

The fish recipes that follow I love, or they wouldn't be here. (They start on page 115.)

## Sherry Chicken (Serves 6)

4 whole chicken breasts, skinned, split, preferably not boned,
                    arranged in shallow, buttered baking dish.
1 can Cream of Chicken soup (regular size)  
1 can Cream of Mushroom soup   "    "     } Mix and pour  
1 can Cream of Celery soup      "    "     } over chicken.  
1 cup sherry                               } Bake, uncovered 2½ to 3
                                             hours at 325°

This is the canned soup routine carried to its zenith. Don't disdain. It's delicious. The only effort involved is with the can opener.

Serve with rice or mashed potato—anything in which you can make a "well" to receive the elegant juices.

## Wrap-up Chicken   (for super-informal, no-work fare.)

① Tear off squares of heavy-duty foil, one per person. Butter an ample area of each sheet.

② At center of each sheet place any cut of chicken your heart desires, skin side down.

③ Paint chicken with melted butter. Salt and pepper it to taste.

④ Pile up on or around the chicken any or all of the following: slices of potato (skin and all), carrot sticks, celery sticks, slice of tomato, strips of green pepper, slice of onion. Wrap up firmly.

⑤ Place on cookie sheet in preheated 400° oven for 1 hour or 325° for 2 hours.

That's all there is to it. Better serve some nice crusty bread to sop up juices.

"Marie Hays' Chicken Casserole (serves 12 generously—
more, if dainty diners.)

1 onion, chopped
1 heaping cup chopped celery
1 green pepper, chopped
¼ cup chopped pimiento
1 eight-ounce can water chestnuts, sliced
½ pound (8 ounces) sharp Cheddar cheese, grated

} All these ingredients placed in bowl large enough for entire recipe.

1 (10 ¾ ounce) can cream of celery soup
1 cup milk
⅓ cup mayonnaise
juice of ½ lemon
1 teaspoon salt
dash of Tabasco Sauce

} Mix well and stir into above.

1 six-ounce package spinach noodles, cooked according to
directions and stirred into above.

4 cups white meat chicken (you may substitute turkey), cut into
(cooked chicken)     bite-sized pieces and carefully trimmed of
all skin, gristle, etc. One can never be too
careful in this area. It makes all the difference.
Stir carefully into above so as not to break
pieces.

4 cups coarse bread crumbs } Mix and then sprinkle over
¼ pound butter, melted       all of above which has been
transferred to a large, shallow
baking dish or pan which has
been buttered.

Bake, uncovered, in preheated 350° oven for 45 minutes.
It is attractive served in squares.
Make it a day ahead and your party is nearly ready.
Of the thousands of chicken casserole recipes, I put
this one near the top of the list. Some variety of
tomato salad is suggested as an accompaniment.

# Crunchy Chicken Casserole

(As served by Peg Funkhauser at a memorable dinner. She says this will serve 6 youthful appetites or 8 older restrained diners.)

2 cups cooked chicken in bite-sized pieces
1 cup chopped celery
1 cup slivered almonds
1 cup thinly sliced water chestnuts

} Toss together

½ cup mayonnaise
½ cup sour cream
1 cup cream of chicken soup

} Mix

Stir all this together and pour into buttered 2 quart casserole. Cover, bake for 3/4 hour at 325°.

This recipe does not call for salt. But add some if you feel the need. It is a recipe that improves by being made up a day ahead of time, refrigerated, then baked after company arrives.

I like to serve this with rice mixed with pineapple chunks and any plain green vegetable such as peas, green beans, or zucchini, in contrast to the richness of the chicken. This all adds up to an outstandingly delicious repast that is a cinch to make.

# Chicken or Turkey Divan (Serves 8)

~ An old Luncheon dish standby ~

Butter a shallow, proper-sized baking dish to hold what follows.

2 (ten ounce) packages frozen broccoli or asparagus,
    or the equivalent thereof in garden-fresh, just barely
    cooked and well drained. Arrange one of these
    vegetables in bottom of baking dish.

slices of chicken or turkey (2 or 3 slices per person), arranged
    over the vegetable.   (Cooked poultry)

2 cans (10¾ ounce) cream of chicken soup
1 cup mayonnaise
1 tablespoon lemon juice       } Mix and spread
½ teaspoon curry                  over above.

sharp Cheddar cheese, grated, and spread over all in amount
                to suit your fancy.
Bake in preheated 325° oven, uncovered, for about
½ hour or until sauce bubbles nicely.

This dish seems to call for a light salad such as pear halves
with sweet onion rings and a French-type dressing (page 138).
No mayonnaise or creamy dressing. Or how about grapefruit
and avocado with Poppy Seed Dressing? (page 138)
I'd also serve hot, crusty rolls of some sort. And as you've
run the gamut of meat, cheese, vegetable, fruit, greens — dessert
might be a delicate baked custard and a crisp cookie. Cranberry
juice and ginger ale (half and half) served in wine glasses would be both
the right color and taste note to go with this meal, unless you prefer wine,
in which case a rosé would be attractive.

# New Canaan Chicken Livers (serves 8)

4 tablespoons butter, heated in large skillet

2 onions, chopped and sautéed lightly in butter. Remove from
     skillet and put aside.

2 pounds chicken livers that have been cut in half and nicely trimmed
     of all connective tissue. Shake livers in a bag of flour,
     salt and pepper until well coated. Sauté in same
     pan about 3 minutes. Remove and put aside with onions.

½ pound mushrooms, sliced ⎫ Put in skillet and cook until bacon is
½ pound bacon, chopped ⎬ crisp. If too much fat, pour off some,
     ⎭ leaving enough to absorb:

2 tablespoons of flour in which liver was shaken. Remove
     from heat and add slowly:

1 cup chicken broth ⎫ Stir constantly. Return to heat and cook
1 cup dry red wine ⎬ and stir for about 3 minutes. Add the
     liver and onions. Serve at once or
     reheat later.

Remember that liver requires brief cooking, otherwise it toughens.
Serve with rice laced with toasted almonds, and have a colorful,
simple vegetable.  Or serve on toast.

# Individual Chicken Pie   (Makes 6 pies)

This recipe tells exactly how chicken pies were made at the Algonquin Hotel* in the days of Frank Case, and let's hope the tradition continues. Never have I tasted their equal. And neither had Irvin S. Cobb, who wrote: "The Algonquin's individual Chicken Potpie has never been bettered and never will be either, until they start making chicken pies with birds of Paradise instead of chickens."

Make this rich, glorious pastry a day ahead so you are ready to orchestrate the whole:

1 cup cold butter (½ pound), chopped into small pieces and cut into
2 cups flour  with knives or pastry blender, lightly, thoroughly.
           Then add gradually
½ cup ice water, chopping away until incorporated .
               Pat together into a large ball, wrap in
               plastic and refrigerate overnight. This
               is important.

It's also smart to prepare the chicken and vegetables a day ahead, but not a necessity. Here's how:

1 fowl (around 6 pounds) cut up (Try and find a "fowl"! All
               chickens seem to meet an early death these
               days.) Place the best bird you can find
               in a pot along with the following:

* In the theatre district of New York City.

2 whole carrots
2 onions
3 or 4 whole stalks celery
1 gallon (4 quarts) water
1 bay leaf
2 cloves
1½ tablespoons salt

Bring to a boil, cooking until fowl is tender, but testing the vegetables early on and removing them the minute they start to be fork tender. Put them aside to cool.

When the bird is cooked, strain off the broth and chill it for easy fat removal. Cut up the chicken into good-sized, clear pieces of meat. (If you're careless about trimming the meat, don't bother to make the pies.) Refrigerate meat, broth, and vegetables until next day or proceed with recipe as follows:

Put some white meat and some dark meat in each of 6 buttered individual baking bowls or casseroles. Top the meat with daintily cut-up cooked celery, onions, carrots. (This embellishes more than overwhelms. The chicken matters most.)

Now create the gravy in which all is immersed:

⅓ cup butter (¼ pound stick), melted
¾ cup flour, stirred into butter
5 cups chicken broth (fat removed), stirred slowly into above roux. Cook and stir 10 minutes. Then add:

1 cup cream
juice of ½ lemon
salt, to taste

Stir well into above. Pour into the 6 bowls.

Now for the pastry crust. Cut the well-chilled pastry into 6 parts. Roll out into thin circles. Arrange on each pie dish, crimping edges and piercing top with sharp fork, for escape of steam. Bake in preheated 450° oven for 10 minutes. Then turn oven down to 350° and continue baking until crust nicely browned. Watch it!

One more warning about the little pies:
Place them on a cookie sheet lined with foil.
Pies are inclined to bubble over.

You may make one big pie if it suits you better.

A friend brought me some partridges one day. I treated them just as indicated in the foregoing recipe (soaking them first in baking soda and water, then rinsing). The results were spectacular.

This is old-fashioned, buttery, country cookin'. It does not fall in the quick and easy to prepare category, but is worth every bit of effort in achieving its straightforward, uncluttered excellence. Should you have seduction in mind, get to work and serve this dish.

Frank Case hasn't recommended this but I do: Make a brown paper template the size of your pie dish top. Cut pastry according to this pattern and bake on cookie sheet while pie or pies are heating. Watch it. It will brown quickly and crisps on both sides. Place on pie or pies when ready to serve. This seems an improvement, though you can't lose either way.

Bertha Rose's  Roast Chicken  sans labor

Place a 3 or 4 pound chicken in greased pan.
Anoint with lemon juice and onion salt inside and out.
Bake in preheated 400° oven for 1 hour - and no peeking!

That's it.

This may be served in countless ways, according to
what you enjoy with chicken. When doing it this quick
way I tend to serve it with spaghetti, a tomato sauce,
green salad, crusty bread — a most satisfying meal all in
an hour's time.      Or refrigerate the bird to be ready
for sandwiches, salads, casseroles.     And don't forget
to simmer the carcass for a fine broth.

"Because Napoleon did not like to wait and had no
fixed hours of eating, his chef had a roast chicken
ready every fifteen minutes."
                                    Barbara Norman
                                    Tales of the Table

# Chicken Breasts with Grapes (serves 4)

4 half breasts chicken, boned, skin on (fairly large breasts).
butter and touch of vegetable oil, heated in 10 inch skillet.
 Add breasts, skin side down, and brown
 slowly, sprinkling with half of following
 mixture:
1 teaspoon salt, ½ teaspoon paprika, ¼ teaspoon pepper, ¼ teaspoon
 crushed rosemary

 When breasts are nicely browned, turn them over
 and add the following:
1 small onion, finely chopped
1 chicken bouillon cube dissolved in      } Mix and spoon over
½ cup boiling water                            chicken. Then sprinkle
½ cup rose' wine                              on remaining salt mixture.
                                             } Cover and simmer until
                                  chicken is cooked and tender
                                  (10 to 20 minutes).

 Remove chicken to warm serving dish.
 Into the same skillet and its good juices add:
1 tablespoon cornstarch mixed with ) Cook, stirring gently,
1 tablespoon cold water              } until sauce boils and
                                   thickens. Then add
½ cup red grapes, halved and seeded.
 Pour sauce over chicken and serve at once.
 Or you may hold sauce and chicken
 separately, if you prefer this done ahead,
 and reheat quickly and combine when
 ready to eat.

 (You may substitute white wine and white grapes.)

# Oriental Drumsticks (serves 4)

8 chicken drumsticks, nestled side by side in buttered baking dish.

¼ cup soy sauce

3 tablespoons dark brown sugar

2 tablespoons lemon juice

2 tablespoons sherry

1 Tablespoon salad oil

1 teaspoon powdered ginger

⅓ cup chopped green onions

1 garlic clove, minced

Mix and pour over drumsticks. Cover and refrigerate at least 3 hours, but better overnight. Turn in the marinade at least once. Bake in the marinade in preheated 350° oven, uncovered, for about 1½ hours, Turning once during baking.

These browned, tender drumsticks may be served hot or cold. They are unbeatable as picnic fare. They are so easy to make that a child can do it. My granddaughter did, with obvious pride, when she was only nine. Kids love them.

". . . . . poultry is for the cook what canvas is for the painter."
Brillat-Savarin

# Roast Turkey Breast

Place turkey breast in a deep <u>covered</u> casserole, having first buttered the casserole and put some onion slices in the bottom, on which the turkey may rest. Sprinkle the breast with some <u>salt</u> and <u>Bell's Poultry Seasoning</u>. Bake in a <u>325° oven</u> until tender. No need to baste. Being covered, it does not dry out, yet the skin of the breast browns nicely. Length of baking depends on weight. The breasts often come frozen, and the wrapper indicates baking time. I always extend their estimate. (<u>½ hour per pound</u> is about my way.) The bird exudes the most heavenly juices. Save them! Don't dare throw them out; they are pure gold and contain practically no fat. Save the onions also, blending into broth for whatever use.

To make gravy out of the juice, place it in blender with some flour (<u>1 cup juice</u> to <u>2 level tablespoons of flour</u>). Stir on stove until thickened, salting by the addition of a <u>chicken bouillon cube</u> or more as needed.

If you don't require gravy, refrigerate the oniony broth (or freeze it) as a basis for various excellent soups or to enhance a white sauce for creamed turkey. Also, when the breast carcass is available, break it up and simmer it to leach out more broth.

The first time the turkey appears on the table, hot and freshly baked, I probably serve gravy, but if not, then I serve a creamed vegetable with it. But never both, as that would make too runny a dinner plate.

Turkey is a relatively fat-free, highly digestible

meat, and the modern accessibility of just the breast is a boon to both the cook and the health-conscious.

To face a weekend of guests, nothing can fill the bill better than a turkey breast — meaning not only one easy hot dinner but leftovers of white meat for sandwiches, salads, casseroles, soups, creamed turkey or whatever. One finds it in the market twelve months a year.

# Grape-Stuffed Cornish Hens   (serves 4)

<u>4 hens</u>, washed. If they contain giblets, simmer them in water
　　　　　seasoned with <u>chicken bouillon cubes</u>.
　　　　　Line up hens in shallow, <u>buttered</u> pan,
　　　　　filling each one with

<u>seedless white grapes</u> ～ Stuff the hens <u>full</u> and skewer
　　　　　cavity opening so that grapes stay put.

<u>salt</u> and <del>pepper</del> hens and place them in <u>preheated</u>
　　　　　350°oven for an <u>hour or more</u>. Legs
　　　　　should move easily when done and
　　　　　birds should be well browned.

<u>¼ pound butter, melted</u>　⎫
<u>4 tablespoons parsley flakes</u>　⎬ Mix and spoon over or
<u>2 tablespoons dried tarragon</u>　⎭ brush on birds at least
　　　　　　　　　　　twice while baking,
　　　　　　　　　　　until all used up.

———————

You may do all this at the last minute, but with my
company-ready hang-up here's how I do it. I roast
the birds in the morning and then, when sufficiently
cooled for handling, I cut them in half with duck
shears and arrange them on a <u>buttered</u> stove-to-table
platter or shallow baking dish, the halves resting over
the grapes. Keep the hens whole if you want, but I
feel they are easier to handle this way. Forget them
until the dinner hour. When almost ready to serve,
place birds in <u>preheated</u> 400°oven until well heated.
<u>About 10 minutes</u> does the job. Decorate with plenty
of parsley.
　　　　　The above method allows you to have

gravy with no last-minute panic. The birds exude the most succulent juices. I strain this juice from the first roasting pan, along with the broth from the giblets, and refrigerate it until the fat hardens on top. (For greater speed, use the freezer.) Remove fat, measure juice and put in blender. In the proportion of 1 cup juice to 2 tablespoons flour, blend and transfer to double boiler. (You may stretch with some water if necessary.) Cook and stir in double boiler until thickened and smooth. Put aside to reheat just before serving, having corrected seasoning. Nothing could be easier or better. This type of gravy is neither fattening nor indigestible — just a good, nourishing broth with excellent flavor. Rice goes well with Cornish hens and makes a fine receptacle for the gravy.

I cook all poultry and roast lamb in the fashion described above if I want to be company-ready — and who doesn't? It also makes gravy possible, a chore that is anathema to all of us if made just before serving. In fact, one seldom sees it presented these days, more's the pity. I figure it is because of the dread of that last-minute ordeal, plus the dieter's fear of added poundage. If gravy is made by the old-fashioned roux method, loaded with animal fat, it should be avoided. But by the procedure described above, it is not only conveniently ready, but harmless to dyspeptic and dieter alike. And it adds immeasurably to the deliciousness of certain meals.

P.S. Concerning the Cornish hen giblets, they are so small I don't bother to cut them up for the gravy (as with chicken or turkey) but use them to make a broth and then strain them out. However, if ambition allows, go ahead and cut up the tiny things.

# Roast Wild Duck   (Plan ½ duck per serving)

①  Soak ducks in plenty of cold water (with a handful of baking soda mixed in) for several hours or overnight. Rinse thoroughly.

②  Stuff each duck with salt, pepper, a good teaspoon of dried rosemary (more if fresh), part of an onion, part of an apple with skin on, some cut up celery along with the leaves.

③  Place in large buttered pan and paint each duck liberally with concentrated orange juice. Cover with foil and bake in preheated 350° oven for at least 2 hours. Allow to cool a bit.

④  When cool enough to handle, cut each duck in half with duck shears. Discard stuffing. Arrange each half skin side up on buttered stove-to-table platter (if you have one, otherwise return to same pan from which you have saved the juices). Baste the ducks with pan juices, more orange concentrate, more salt and pepper. At this point they can wait most of the day. Here is the next step, either delayed or at once, according to your schedule:

⑤  Place in preheated 400° oven for 20 minutes or so until heated and skin somewhat crisp. Remove from oven and have this glaze ready:

⑥  Some currant jelly and a dash of sherry heated and stirred until jelly melts. Paint this on the duck with a brush to give it a pleasant sheen.

⑦  Garnish all with mandarin orange sections and parsley.

~~~~~~~~~~~~~~~~~~~~

There are those who prefer their duck, wild or domestic, with blood running. I'm sufficiently unsophisticated to like it this way better, lots better.

~~~~~~~~~~~~~~~~~~~~

# Roast Quail    (serves 6 to 8)

A lot of quail is eaten in the South, some only barely cooked. I go to the other extreme, not liking slippery birds. My method always seemed to please. Hope it will please you. Despite long cooking it is not dry, just tender.

Quail may be presoaked in a soda and water solution, if you prefer, to remove the gamy taste. Then rinse well. Or soak in plain or salted water to hydrate them. (Soak 1 or 2 hours.)

Dry off 8 or 10 quail and arrange in buttered, shallow baking dish of stove-to-table variety. Anoint with the juice of 2 lemons, yes, 2. Then mask with 2 cans Campbell's Cream of Chicken soup, regular size. No more seasonings. Place in preheated 325° oven for at least 2 hours, or until quail are nicely browned on top and pan juices a bit crusty. Putting under broiler a minute or so helps the browning, if necessary. Baste now and then during the roasting in an uncovered baking dish.

Serve in same dish, garnished with parsley. Good served with wild rice (page 152) well laced with mushrooms and onions that have been sautéed in butter. Winter squash would go well with this. Currant jelly is ever a treat with game.

# Crown Roast of Pork (serves 8 or more)

For a really fancy party on a cold winter night this is your dish. A visit with your butcher is called for. The usual crown roast consists of the rib sections of two pork loins. The butcher can supply you with the frilly coverings with which to top each rib when ready to serve.

Butter your roasting pan and sprinkle liberally with flour (this makes browner, tastier gravy). Place crown roast therein. Salt and pepper it. Then fill the center of roast with Cranberry Stuffing (page 285). Place in preheated 325° oven and allow about 45 minutes per pound, uncovered, no basting necessary (probably around 3½ hours or more). My advice is to turn a deaf ear to some modern cooks who recommend pink pork. Ugh.

When roast has cooked long enough to have produced some nice, brown, crusty juices in the pan, remove roast from oven and from pan. You may place roast in another buttered roasting pan and return it to oven, or put it aside until initial pan is free. If contents of roasting pan is reduced to all fat — pour it off. Otherwise place pan on burner and reduce until it is all fat. Discard all fat and pour some water in the pan. Boil and scrape until liquid is nice and brown. While this simmers, put water and flour in blender in proportion of 1 cup water to 1½ tablespoons flour. Blend well and pour slowly into roasting pan, stirring vigorously. (You be the judge of how much gravy you want.) Add salt and pepper to taste. Transfer this luscious, fat-free gravy to a double boiler. Cover and forget it until ready to reheat at serving time. (Nothing worse than trying to make gravy after guests have arrived.)

Having made the gravy, return roast to oven (if you haven't already done so) to complete roasting time you have figured out it needs. Give the roast about 15 minutes' rest after removing from oven and before carving. This will give you time to place the frilly cuffs on each rib and to surround roast with whatever your artistic bent suggests: parsley/radish roses/carrot curls/cherry tomatoes/fruits. Or how about a raw cranberry necklace? Tableau.

Where there's gravy, potatoes are imperative. My favorite way with pork is to boil potatoes with white turnips (half and half), then mash as for regular mashed potatoes. This can be done in the morning, plopped into a buttered soufflé dish and heated quickly just before serving. Then, of course, side dishes of apple sauce and some cole slaw. Or skip that and serve a Waldorf Salad (page 143). Have cooked vegetables that are plain and colorful. For dessert I'd choose something light and lovely such as Snow Pudding (page 266) or Prune Whip (page 263). Pork need not be a heavy meal if you make fat-free gravy and are careful of what you serve as accompaniments.

The gravy method described here I recommend for all roasts, not just pork. It has the double advantage of being fat free and completed in advance of meal. Forget the roux method that is universally recommended and loaded with grease.

"Everything in a pig is good.
What ingratitude has permitted
his name to become a term
of opprobrium?"
grimod de la Reyniere

# Dorothy's Dixie Pork Chops  (serves 6 to 8)

8 pork chops, trimmed of as much fat as possible. Rub a piece of
fat trimming in heated skillet, remove, add chops,
browning on both sides. Remove chops and place
in one layer in buttered, shallow baking dish.

Salt, sprinkled over all

Sage, sprinkled over all

4 tart apples, sliced with skins on. Remove every vestige of core.
Cover the chops with the apple slices.

Brown sugar, sprinkled over apples in judicious amount.

1½ cups water ⎫ Blend in blender and pour into pan
in which you browned the chops.
1 tablespoon vinegar ⎬ Stir and scrape up all the good of the
browning. When smooth and thickened,
3 tablespoons flour ⎭ toss in

¾ cup (about) raisins  and spoon this sauce over each chop.
Cover with foil (or pan's own cover) and
bake in preheated 350° oven for 1 hour.

You may do all this ahead of time if more convenient.
As the dinner hour approaches, give it another ½ hour at 350°,
still covered. Or if one lingers over cocktails, give it
another hour at 250°. Remove cover. Turn oven to
400° for around 10 minutes for slight browning if you
think it needs it. Optional.

A southern favorite. No wonder.

Be sure to serve mashed potatoes with this dish to receive
some of the good meat juices.

# Judy's Sweet and Sour Pork Chops

<u>pork chops</u> ~ best center cut, trimmed of as much fat as possible.
(about 1 inch)
thick      Arrange in buttered,* shallow baking dish.

{ <u>salt</u>
{ <u>pepper</u>, freshly ground ~ sprinkled over chops.

<u>lemons</u> ~ cut paper-thin <u>slices</u> and place one on each chop after
           you have anointed each chop with lemon <u>juice</u>.
<u>onions</u> ~ a generous slice placed on top of lemon.
{ <u>ketchup</u> ~ mix together about ⅓ brown sugar and
{ <u>brown sugar</u>    ⅔ ketchup and spread carefully over each chop.

        Cover the whole dish securely with foil if cover is
lacking. You may do this a day ahead or a few hours.
(Letting it marinate somewhat is desirable but not vital.)
Bake <u>covered</u> in preheated <u>350°</u> oven for <u>2 hours</u>. Uncover,
baste with pan juices a couple of times as you continue to bake,
<u>uncovered</u>, for about another half hour — until juices are about
evaporated and chops nice and brown. Moist, tender, delicious.

        Be sure to serve with mashed or baked potato and apple sauce
and cole slaw and a plain, unadorned vegetable. If you are a zealous
forehanded buff you may cool and <u>freeze</u> the chops after the two-hour cooking
and have them party-ready way ahead. Then thaw and give that last half hour
or so just before serving.

* When it comes to serving and/or washing the pan, you'll be glad you
buttered it. Helps prevent sticking.

# Quick Sweet and Sour Pork or Chicken (serves 4 to 6)

2 tablespoons oil (I use corn oil.)
butter - just a dab for flavor } heated in good-sized skillet

1 green pepper, coarsely cut up
1 onion, coarsely chopped
2 garlic cloves, minced } Stir-fry 2 or 3 minutes in above oil. Then remove from pan.

1 pound (about) pork or chicken breast, cut into very thin strips and free of all fat, bones, skin } Stir fry in same pan around 3 minutes or until meat browns a bit. Salt it slightly. Then add the following:

juice from one 8 ounce can pineapple chunks (unsweetened) with sufficient water added to make 1 cup

2 tablespoons corn starch

½ cup maple syrup

¼ cup cider vinegar

3 tablespoons soy sauce

2 tablespoons ketchup

Stir this all together and then pour into the browned meat. Add the pineapple chunks and the green pepper-onion mixture. Stir constantly, allowing to come to boil for one minute. Serve at once, or cool and reheat when ready to eat. Serve over rice.

I like to keep a good cut of lean pork and breasts of chicken in the freezer — ready for creating this easy dish.

# Swiss Ham Casserole (serves 8)

2 cups (8 ounces) shredded Swiss cheese  Mix ½ cup of this cheese
with

½ cup buttered bread crumbs and hold.

½ cup chopped green onions ⎫ Mix with remaining 1½ cups
1 tablespoon dried dill weed ⎬ of cheese.    Hold.

2 tablespoons butter ⎫
2 Tablespoons flour ⎬  Make a white sauce.
1 teaspoon salt ⎪  (see pages 162 and 163)
2 cups milk ⎭

4 good-sized boiled potatoes (unsalted), cut into small cubes or
thin slices.

3 cups cooked ham (cubed)

In a buttered baking dish, layer:
⅓ of the potatoes
½ of the ham
½ of the cheese-onion-dill mixture
½ of the sauce
Repeat, ending with potatoes.
Top with cheese-bread crumb mixture.

Bake uncovered in 350° oven  30 to 35 minutes.
Improves by standing a bit before serving.
A fine way to make use of leftover ham.
Its' the dill that makes it different.
(Should you be blessed with fresh dill, use 3 tablespoons of the chopped herb.)

# Ham Loaf Caramel (serves 6)

<u>3 eggs</u>, beaten in a good-sized bowl. To the eggs add

<u>1¼ cups milk</u>

<u>5 slices bread</u>, crumbled into egg and milk mixture. Then add

<u>½ teaspoon salt</u> and

<u>½ teaspoon dry mustard</u> ⌣ Mix all together thoroughly. Then add

<u>1 pound ham</u>, ground, which has been trimmed of all fat. Then add

<u>½ pound best round steak</u>, ground. Stir the meat into egg mixture with zeal.

<u>½ cup dark brown sugar</u>) Mix and place in bottom of well buttered
<u>¼ teaspoon ground cloves</u>) loaf pan or ring mold or separate custard cups. Then pack in the meat mixture.

Bake in preheated 350° oven, uncovered, for <u>one hour</u>. Unmold onto warm platter. (Assist the process by running knife around edge of molds.) Garnish with parsley or something for eye appeal.

This ham loaf goes well with baked sweet potatoes or yams, and with Farmer's Cabbage (page 172). A pineapple or Waldorf salad is a fine accompaniment, or just some nice cold pineapple chunks pepped up with a touch of sherry, or some apple sauce. Apple and/or pineapple, in some form, belong with ham.

# Effortless Beef Dinner (serves 4)
## (Kindness of Gladys Thompson)

1 pound <u>slice</u> of round steak, trimmed of all fat and either
cubed or cut into thin strips as in Beef Stroganoff,
according to your fancy. Place in buttered casserole dish.

1 can (10¾ ounce) Campbell's Cream of Chicken Soup (yes, <u>chicken</u>)
Pour soup over beef and mix well. <u>Cover</u>!
Place in <u>250° oven</u> for <u>5 hours</u>. Forget it until
time to serve.

Do not be tempted to doctor up this dish in any way. No salt,
nothing. You may want to pat off (just before serving) a
little fat that may rise to the top, with a paper towel or one
of those small mops made for fat-banishing purposes.

    This recipe may be multiplied endlessly —
an easy road to success for a crowd. It's also satisfactory
if cooking for one. Put what is not eaten into 3 or 4
freezer-to-stove-to-table ramekins. It freezes well and the main
dish is ready ahead. Serve with mashed or baked potato or rice
or noodles that go so well with the luscious gravy this slow cooking produces.
Broiled tomatoes make a fine accompaniment as does a crisp green salad.

    Having said not to doctor up this recipe a friend of mine did.
She added about ¾ cup Burgundy. It was an improvement.
So I copied her and then went one better and added 1 teaspoon Sidney's
Seasoning (page 286) in addition to the wine. More improvement.

But I can also recommend the original two-ingredient recipe.

## Beef Tenderloin
### (A hurry-up method)

Place whole or half tenderloin, which has been brought to room temperature (!), in oiled baking pan. Anoint it with a little butter or oil, a dusting of flour, some onion or garlic salt and some pepper. Roast in preheated 450° oven for exactly 20 minutes. Remove from pan, place on cutting board or platter and allow to rest for about 10 minutes before carving into lovely slices — pink inside, a bit crusty outside.

Serve with Chattanooga Sauce (page 269) or Horseradish Gel (page 270)

I'm chronically torn between the above fast method of cooking a tenderloin and the one described in my previous book (325° for one hour). You can't lose either way.

One thinks of tenderloin as too expensive to indulge in. Relax and consider that it's the most fat-free beef you can buy, so you'll save on trips to the doctor or reducing salon; it's bone-free, so there is not a scrap of waste; it's effortless to prepare, is totally tender and delicious and sure to make everyone happy. While you're buying it, concentrate on the astronomical cost of the mediocre meal you recently had at a restaurant and know that by staying home and eating tenderloin, you're really saving money.

# Ethel's* Empress Beef  (serves 4)

about ½ pound best beef (either fresh or leftover roast or steak), cut into julienne strips, cleared of all fat and gristle and browned ever so slightly in

3 tablespoons vegetable oil in pan large enough for whole recipe. Remove seared beef from pan and then add the following:

3 stalks celery, cut on bias

1 large sweet onion, thinly sliced

mushrooms, sliced fresh or canned, a heaping cup or so

½ cup water chestnuts, sliced, or more if you desire

¼ pound green beans, French cut, fresh or frozen

or

¼ pound snow peas, fresh or frozen

Salt, a touch only. Soy sauce that follows is salty.

*Stir-fry for a few minutes, scraping up the good brown meat residue. Then cover and simmer slowly about 3 minutes. (Vegetables should be crunchy, not mushy.) Lastly add the meat. You may hold now or go on to next step and serve at once.*

1 tablespoon cornstarch
½ tablespoon sugar
½ cup water
5 tablespoons soy sauce**

*Mix this and have ready for the last minute when the above is heated for serving (just heated, no more!) Pour over all and stir until it thickens and shines and coats all. Serve with rice.*

This is one of my favorites for leftover beef. It turns a leftover into company fare. Here's what I served with it recently and everyone seemed happy:
Empress Beef
Rice (page 152)
Zucchini and Tomatoes Niçoise (page 199)   Cole Slaw (page 139 or 143)
Melba Pears (page 260)   Hermits (page 235)

* From the kitchen of Ethel Reinhart Congleton (A great cook.)
** I like Kikkoman Soy Sauce best.

# Rancher's Hash   (Serves 6)

(I use this recipe the most often for leftover beef from a roast or steak or whatever. One of my favorite meals.)

1 onion
4 ribs celery
1 green pepper
} chopped and sautéed slightly in:

2 Tablespoons vegetable oil — or half oil, half butter
1½ pounds (about) ground beef, fresh or leftover, sautéed lightly
with above. Then add:

2 teaspoons chili powder (or all you want, according to taste) and
16 ounce can tomatoes   and simmer about 10 minutes.
salt, added to taste
1½ cups cooked rice
} Stir into above and transfer to
buttered, shallow baking dish.
¾ cup sharp grated Cheddar cheese, sprinkled over the top.

This is ready to bake at once or to hold as long as you want. Slide into preheated 375° oven, uncovered, and bake until thoroughly heated and cheese bubbly, around 20 minutes.

Lena's   Hungarian Cabbage Rolls

1 pound good ground beef
  (or half beef, half pork)
1 egg
¾ cup uncooked rice          Mix this all together thoroughly.
1 good-sized onion, finely chopped
  and sautéed slightly in butter.
Salt and pepper (be generous)

1 head cabbage, center core dug out somewhat. Dip in boiling
    water to aid in removing leaves. Keep dipping
    until you have broken off about 12 nice leaves.
    Cut hard ends off of leaves so easier to manipulate.
    Put 1/12 of meat mixture in center of each leaf
    and fold leaves into nice neat packages (but not too
    firmly so rice can expand) and place, seam side down,
    in kettle or casserole in which you cook them.
    ( Not in aluminum!)

2 tablespoons butter
2 tablespoons flour    Make a roux. Remove from heat
                       and stir in
2 cups tomato juice, slowly and until lump-free along with
1 tablespoon brown sugar
        Pour this tomato sauce over the cabbage rolls. It should
    cover them. If not, add some water or tomato juice.
    Cover. Bring to simmer. Let simmer slowly for
    about 1 hour. Careful not to scorch. I avoid the
    danger of burning by placing cabbage rolls in
    buttered casserole, covering and baking in
    325° oven for 1 hour from the time it starts to bubble.

When Lena's mother, Mrs. Marcus, made these cabbage rolls in Phillipsburg, New Jersey, back in the 1930's, the whole neighborhood got wind of it, literally. They waft one fine odor while cooking. It was always an event for rejoicing for she shared her rolls with her neighbors, making hundreds of rolls at a time in a huge kettle on her coal-burning iron stove. An iron stove with its gently diffused heat made safe simmering possible. I prefer the oven method in this day and age, and one can bring the casserole right to the table.

The simplicity of this Hungarian dish is appealing and it can well stand alone for the main course with just some crusty bread as accompaniment. But a green salad, well laced with herbs, would be a pleasant taste contrast. Maybe fruit and cheese to polish off the meal if in an abstaining mood. Otherwise here's an opportunity to bring forth your most sinful dessert, for cabbage rolls do not fall in the rich food category.

# Chili    (serves 4)

(Kit Carson's alleged dying words: "Wish I had)
(time for just one more bowl of chili.")

1 or 2 tablespoons vegetable oil, heated in kettle large
enough for whole recipe.

1 large onion, cut up and cooked slightly in above oil.

1 pound best ground beef, crumbled into above and browned
slightly along with the onion.
Then add all of the following:

1 regular can red kidney beans

1 two-cup can stewed Tomatoes

1 clove garlic, minced

1 fifteen and ½ ounce bottle Ragú Spaghetti Sauce (plain)
(This is optional but an improvement.)

1 tablespoon chili powder (or more if you like it hot)

Simmer gently for 1 hour, being careful
not to scorch. Taste test and add
salt, if needed, and
paprika, for sure.        Serve chili in bowls.

This recipe may be multiplied endlessly for a crowd. Freezes well.
Hot homemade corn bread or muffins go beautifully
with chili, though many just serve crackers.
Cole slaw or finger greens accompany well.
Chili is the perfect standby that is ready to serve
at any old hour. All you need do is heat it up.

## Marion Curto's Meat Loaf (Serves 8)

In a large mixing bowl put:

1 egg
1 tablespoon brown sugar
1 teaspoon salt
1/4 teaspoon freshly ground pepper
1/2 teaspoon dried basil (or a heaping tablespoon of chopped fresh)
1/2 teaspoon dried thyme    " "    "    "    "    "    "    "
2 teaspoons prepared mustard
1/4 cup ketchup
1/2 cup chopped celery
1/2 cup chopped onion
1 1/2 cups stale bread crumbs
2 beef bouillon cubes, dissolved in
1 cup boiling water
1 cup shredded sharp Cheddar cheese
2 pounds ground beef

Simply toss in all above ingredients in order given.
Mix thoroughly with clean hands.
Place on buttered stove-to-table platter and pat into nice loaf.
Bake in preheated 375° oven for 70 minutes.
This is a 5-star meat loaf!
If you're lucky enough to have any leftover,
it makes excellent sandwiches.

### Emma Lou's Hot Dogs

The following treatment makes hot dogs taste like the best kosher frankfurters:

① Get the best beef franks.

② Put water in a saucepan and to it add:
      1 teaspoon garlic powder
      1 tablespoon dill weed
      plenty of paprika (to redden hot dogs)

③ Bring water to simmer and then add the hot dogs. Simmer about 5 minutes.

Serve as is or brown a bit in a frying pan.
      Emma Lou said, "You'll be surprised." I was.

Now that you have the perfect hot dog, its time to discuss ways of serving same. Opinions vary. I'll do my best.
①. Butter the hot dog rolls and put in 350° oven until heated and a bit crisped on outside.
②. Place hot dogs, slit down the middle the long way, that have been: A. simmered in plain water or as Emma Lou advises above,
      B. both simmered and then browned in pan in a bit of butter,
      C. browned in pan or on outside grill without any precooking.

      (Place hot dogs, prepared as you choose, in heated rolls.)

③ Have ready for self-service:

dill pickles, cut in strips the long way
(to nestle in that slit in the hot dog).
Gulden's mustard (or French's)
(none of your fancy Dijon mustards, please.)
finely chopped sweet onion

If you take the time to prepare hot dogs as instructed above you just might approach the product that is served at "Jimmy's Hot Dog Stand" on the Phillipsburg, New Jersey, side of the old iron bridge that spans the Delaware River to Easton, Pennsylvania. For several generations this humble establishment has been turning the lowly hot dog into an art form. I know grown men who will go fifty miles out of their way to eat one of Jimmy's hot dogs, reenacting one of those rites of their youth which still bears the power to enchant.

The last word has not been said concerning hot dogs (probably never will be). There are those who recommend ketchup, sauerkraut, chili beans or chopped tomato as embellishments. Others scream disapproval. I'd like to end this long harangue on a touchy subject by giving Judy's (my daughter-in-law) way of serving same. My son reluctantly claims it exceeds Jimmy's. An heretical claim but here it is:

①. Butter rolls, wrap in foil and place in oven.
②. Brown hot dogs in butter in frying pan or grill outdoors.
③. Slit dogs lengthwise and place in slit a length of good Cheddar cheese. (Get cheese that looks like ¼ pound stick of butter and cut it into strips.)

④. Place the hot dogs in the heated rolls and return to
oven until the cheese melts, still foil-covered.
(I'd uncover, but that is one of those on-going
arguments between my son and me. He likes
rolls soft. I like them slightly crisped.)

⑤. Then comes the <u>dill pickle</u>, <u>mustard</u> and <u>onion</u>
treatment as previously indicated.
Ravishing.

––––––––––––

All these suggestions are a far cry from a plain
dog slapped into a cold cottony roll which one encounters
too often. There are those who are lulled by the sign on
the frankfurter package, "fully cooked." It won't hurt you,
but neither will it excite, as can a properly prepared
American hot dog. After all, what did Eleanor Roosevelt
choose to serve to King George the sixth and his lovely
Queen when they visited Hyde Park back in World War II
days? HOT DOGS.

––––––––––––

# Baked Tongue (serves 8 or more)

## (A family favorite)

1 smoked beef tongue, brought to a boil in plenty of cold water.
(It may also be pickled or corned variety.)    Simmer, covered, for 3 or 4 hours until good and tender.
Cool in the broth, skin carefully, trim the root end diligently.

2 eggs, beaten
1½ cups bread crumbs } Combine, making a paste, and pat all over the Tongue which has been placed in a buttered roasting pan (so it won't stick). Bake in preheated 350° oven for ½ hour to form a nice crust.

Serve with Wine-Raisin Sauce (page 271).
No salt added to the tongue recipe as it receives sufficient in the curing.   When it comes to accompaniments, treat tongue as you would ham.
Cold leftover tongue makes the most delicious sandwiches.
An excellent meat not served often enough these days.

One of the most wasteful moments in our history was killing buffalo just for the tongue meat. Hundreds of thousands were shipped to the eastern markets, bringing the hunters 50¢ apiece. Shocking, but suggesting the desirability of tongue as a delicacy.

# Three-way Veal Scallops à la Crème  (serves 4)

__1 pound best veal scallops__, pounded thin, then dried thoroughly.
(If meat is moist, it won't brown well.)

__3 tablespoons butter__ ⎫ Heat in large skillet and then add
__1 tablespoon corn oil__ ⎭ the veal, not crowding it. Brown
meat about 4 minutes on each side.
Remove cooked scallops to a side
dish. Add more butter and oil if
needed.

__3 tablespoons minced green onions__ ⎫ cooked in same
__or shallots__ ⎭ skillet for a minute or
so. Then add to this

__1 tablespoon flour__, and stir it around for another
minute.

Now pour into skillet:

__½ cup dry white wine__
__or white vermouth__ ⎫ Stir and scrape this about
so as to get up all the nice
__½ cup beef bouillon__ ⎬ brown in the pan and to make
__or chicken broth__ ⎭ a lump-free sauce. Then add

__1 cup half and half cream__, stirring well. Allow to simmer
and reduce for about 10 minutes.

__salt and pepper__, added to taste.

You now have a choice of three treatments:

① Leave sauce as is. ⎫ Add the browned scallops
② Add ½ pound cut-up, ⎬ to one of these sauces
sautéed, fresh __mushrooms__. ⎪ and hold until serving
③ Add ½ teaspoon crushed ⎪ time. Cover and bring
__rosemary__ and a squeeze ⎬ to simmer on low heat
of __lemon__. ⎭ for no more than 5 minutes
and serve at once.

Irene Dessau's    Veal Tarragon    (serves 4)

1 pound best veal scallops, pounded thin between pieces of waxed paper with wooden mallet, flat of cleaver or rolling pin. Dredge scallops lightly in

flour, salt, pepper

4 Tablespoons butter, heated in large skillet. Brown the scallops nicely in this for about 4 minutes on each side. Use more butter if need be. Remove browned scallops to side dish as they are completed.

¼ cup dry white wine or white vermouth ) Pour this into skillet, simmering and stirring and scraping up all the coagulated juices. Allow to reduce slightly and then add:
½ cup chicken broth )

a squeeze of fresh lemon juice and ) Return veal to these juices. When ready to serve, cover and bring up to heat for 2 or 3 minutes only.
2 teaspoons dried Tarragon (or more if chopped fresh) )

Scallops are ready to serve. Decorate with parsley. Rice and a green vegetable and broiled tomatoes go well with this.

Jimmy Carter's    Catfish and Bass Fillets

(As directed by Rosalynn Carter in her book, First Lady From Plains.)
Cut the fillets in strips like French fries and marinate in Heinz 57
or A1 Sauce for several hours or overnight. When ready to cook,
transfer the fillet strips to a paper bag containing Bisquick or
pancake mix. Shake well to coat the fish. Fry in hot oil.
"Delicious hot or cold", says Rosalynn.
          Jimmy learned this at a fishing camp and in his
1976 campaign actually cooked some on a television talk show. Wish I'd seen it!

---

          Speaking of catfish reminds me of how much that food
is appreciated in Arkansas. Catfish is to an Arkansan what dried cod is to
a Nova Scotian. And the way some of the real, back-country natives can make
the word "cat" into almost a three-syllable word is a source of delight:
"caay-ut-fish."   "Grits" also turns into "greee-uts."
          Southern food brings on the subject of hushpuppies
and my idol, Marjorie Kinnan Rawlings, a hushpuppy enthusiast. The only
thing I hold against her is that she disliked New England Fishcakes*(!) Well,
I'm not that fond of her hushpuppies. At an Arkansas buffet I bit into that
southern specialty thinking it was a fishcake. What a letdown.
She probably had a similar experience in reverse when visiting
in the North.

---

* It's supposed to be a no-no to make reference to my Bentley Farm Cookbook for
fear of frustrating the gentle reader who lacks it. But temptation impels me to
say that I cover exhaustively (and exhaustingly) the subject of the New England Saturday night
banquet of Baked Beans, Steamed Brown Bread and Fish Cakes in that still-available book.
(page 114)

## Boiled Lobster (1 lobster per person is usually enough.)

The best lobster I have ever eaten was at the Ayers' home at Oyster Harbor on Cape Cod. (I think the short cooking time was the answer.) This is the way it was done: Bring a large kettle of water to a boil (with salt or without, 2 teaspoons salt to every quart. I use none). Immerse live and kicking chicken lobsters (under 1½ pounds) into the water, which will cause it to cease boiling. When the water comes up to a full boil again remove the lobsters with tongs. They are ready to serve.

There are those who keep on boiling for 5 to 15 minutes. Take your choice. But one thing to know: The longer lobster cooks, after a certain point, the tougher it gets. So be careful not to spoil one of the great delicacies of the table. According to Harold McGee, the great food scientist, the reason for not overcooking fish or shellfish is that they constitute a special category of meat with fragile connective tissue and low fat which toughens and dries rather than tenderizes with long cooking.

Just for the record, female lobsters are supposed to have a slightly finer flavor than the male. Sorry, I can't tell the difference, but there are those who say they can. Somehow a lobster's sex does not seem crucial.

### Accompaniments to a lobster dinner:

Lobster (or nut) crackers, pointed nut "diggers", regular fork plus tiny fish fork if possible, lobster bibs, scores of paper napkins, one large or individual bowls for discarded shells, finger bowls, melted butter in hot ramekins, lemon wedges. A bit of a free-for-all but fun. With the lobster I like to serve a baked potato or Favorite Potatoes (page 185). Artichokes (page 165) if available, make the perfect vegetable companion for the hot butter and lemon are already at hand for dipping. Cole slaw (page 139 or 142) is another addition to a lobster celebration.

## Instant Seafood Newburg (serves 2 — go on multiplying for a group.)

1 can (10 ¾ ounces) Campbell's Cream of Shrimp Soup, mixed with

3-ounce package softened cream cheese

7 ounces crabmeat, fresh or frozen, picked over carefully,
(about)          discarding any shell, bone, or cartilage.

1 tablespoon sherry

Prepare all this in top of double boiler.
Heat over boiling water when ready to serve.
Best served with rice. Jellied Cucumber would go well
with this ( page 143 ).

~~~~~~~~~

Nancy Sawyer's  ## Baked Fish Fillets

Put fish of your choice on greased foil in a shallow pan.
Cover fillets on both sides with mayonnaise. Sprinkle
generously with buttered Ritz Cracker crumbs.
Bake in preheated 400° oven for 18 minutes.

Serve with lemon wedges.
This has to be the best fish trick I've learned in many a moon.

~~~~~~~~~

Petey Foster's　　　Shrimp Casserole　　(serves 4 to 6)

2 cups chopped fresh raw broccoli, spread over bottom of buttered baking dish.

1 pound shrimp (that has been cooked no more than 1 minute), arranged on broccoli.

1 can Cream of Celery soup (about 10 ounces)

1 cup mayonnaise

1 teaspoon lemon juice

) Mix together and then pour over broccoli and shrimp.

½ cup shredded sharp Cheddar

Pepperidge herbed stuffing (in any amount that pleases you)

} Sprinkled over all as topping.

butter, dotted over all.

Bake, uncovered, in preheated 350° oven for about ½ hour.

# Shrimp Curry   (serves 8)

This is a favorite dish for luncheon or dinner. You may substitute chicken, turkey, crab or lobster for the shrimp. You can't lose.

1 stick (¼ pound) butter, melted in saucepan or top of double boiler.

1 medium onion, chopped ) Sauté in the butter until softened.
1 rib celery, chopped    } Then stir in:

½ cup flour       ) Stir and cook for about 5 minutes
½ teaspoon salt   } so flour does not have raw taste.
1 tablespoon curry ) Remove from heat and stir in:

1 quart whole milk ⌐ slowly, stirring constantly.

(If you are cholesterol casual,       Return to heat and cook and stir
ship in a cup of cream as             until thickened. Careful not to scorch!
part of the quart.)                   (This is where I finish off with
                                      double boiler. I've scorched enough
                                      things to be a little paranoid.)

2 tablespoons sherry, stirred into sauce above.

3 cups shrimp (about), cooked, and added to above only when ready
                        to serve and just to heat through, no more.
                        The longer shrimp is heated the tougher it gets.

Serve with rice and an attractive circle of little bowls containing such traditional embellishments as: finely chopped hard-boiled egg, bacon, nuts, pickles, raw onion, green or ripe olives, shredded coconut, pineapple chunks, chutney (Major Grey's if possible), raisins or currants. Serve some of this or all.
As sauce is deliciously rich, I serve finger greens with cocktails and fruit for dessert.

Medium-sized, uncooked shrimp run about 24 to 1 pound. Right for 4 people.
(See page 30  for cooking directions.)

If you buy shrimp already peeled and cooked, ½ pound will serve 4.

## Butterfly Shrimp (serves 4)

Cut 1 pound of raw shrimp from head to tail on the claw side, but do not cut through the back shell. Remove dark vein. Spread open firmly, butterfly fashion, onto cookie sheet. (There are about 24 medium-sized shrimp to the pound.) Paint some melted butter onto shrimp with pastry brush. Salt lightly. Put under broiler for 4 minutes, then 4 more minutes in a 400° oven. Serve on warm plates with a generous wedge of lemon, some fluffy rice, and a vegetable of your choice. (How about Sautéed Cucumbers on page 174?) This makes a delicate and beautiful meal.

## Scallops — Fast Roasted (Figure ¼ pound per person.)

Rinse and dry bay scallops. Put into bowl and stir in just enough mayonnaise to coat them lightly. Then stir in enough Ritz cracker crumbs to coat them well. Add salt and pepper to taste. Place scallops in a buttered, shallow baking dish, large enough so they are not crowded. Bake in preheated 400° oven for 20 minutes. Wonderful, and not watery as scallops often are. Serve with Tartar Sauce and/or lemon wedges.

Suggested accompaniment: Potato Favorite (page 185), Fondue Tomatoes (page 196), a green salad enhanced with fresh or dried dill.

Merelyn's   Baked Fillets of Sole Piquant   (serves 3)

1 pound fillets of sole, arranged in single layer in shallow dish.

1 cup dry white table wine
    or white vermouth } Pour over fish and add salt to your taste. Allow to marinate ½ hour, no more.

Remove fish from wine. Pat dry and arrange in one layer in buttered, shallow baking dish. Spread fish evenly with the following Topping:

3/4 cup mayonnaise
½ cup grated Parmesan cheese
2 tablespoons grated onion
2 teaspoons lemon juice } Mix, then spread on fillets.

fine, dry bread crumbs
paprika } sprinkled over all.

Bake in preheated 500° oven for about 10 minutes and no more than 12. Crumbs should be nicely browned.
Serve with lemon wedges.

Boiled new potatoes with parsley butter, spinach garnished with hard-boiled eggs, and tomatoes (raw or cooked) all go well with sole. So do cucumbers in any guise.

This recipe will serve 4 of my light-eating friends. But it is customary to serve 1½ pounds of sole for 4 people with heartier appetites.

# Deviled Tuna   (Serves 4)

4 tablespoons butter, melted in saucepan

4 tablespoons flour, stirred into butter and cooked a minute
or more. Remove from heat and add:

1 cup milk
½ cup light cream } stirred slowly into above. Return to heat,
stirring constantly until thickened. Remove
from heat again and add:

2 tablespoons lemon juice

¼ cup sherry

¼ teaspoon dry mustard

1 teaspoon Worcestershire Sauce

1 can best white tuna fish
(water packed, about 7 ounces)

3 hard-boiled eggs, chopped
salt and pepper, to taste

Place all in buttered
casserole or
4 individual baking
dishes.

Top with:

a thin slice of lemon per person and
paprika, sprinkled on the lemon.

Bake in preheated 375° oven about 20 minutes.
(Don't overcook or the eggs might toughen.)

# IV

## Egg — Cheese

## About Eggs

"Tell me, cooks, bakers, and grocers,
Farmers, gardeners, and housewives,
Have you any food more versatile?
Have you any treasure to compare with the egg?"

Mary C. Ferris

## How To Know A Good Egg

Put the egg in a deep utensil of cold water. If fresh it will fall to the bottom, and the faster it falls the fresher it is. A bad egg will float on top. One Hannah Glasse discovered this around 1750. She was scientifically correct.

There is a persistent belief today among health buffs that a fertilized brown egg is better for one than an unfertilized white one. "Neither the shell nor the fertilization of the ovum has any nutritional significance."*

The only unhappy thing about an egg is the high cholesterol content of the yolk. So moderation should be the rule. However, along with seeds and milk, the egg is the most nutritious food on earth, mother nature having designed these three wonders to support life.

---

* On Food and Cooking by Harold McGee

# About Eggs — continued

<u>Slow cooking</u> is the secret with eggs in any form.

The <u>greenish-gray discoloration</u> on the outside of the yolk of a hard-boiled egg is harmless but unaesthetic. To avoid this, cook the eggs barely at a <u>simmer for ½ hour</u>. <u>Never bring to a hard boil.</u>

For <u>ease of peeling</u> a hard-boiled egg, <u>immerse it in cold water</u> immediately after removing it from its simmering bath. <u>Peel at once</u>, or when cool enough to handle! Another trick is to add <u>salt</u> to the water in which eggs are cooked. Shells come off more easily. One comforting thought, when an egg is hard <u>to peel</u>, is that the difficulty arises due to its freshness. An old egg is a cinch to <u>peel</u>.

<u>Beating egg whites</u> successfully is an art. Have them at <u>room temperature</u>. They'll foam better. (This is just the opposite of whipping cream, where bowl, beater and cream should be thoroughly chilled.) In separating whites from yolks it is more easily done with a chilled egg. So <u>plan ahead</u> so as to allow time for whites to come to room temperature. The time-honored custom has been to beat whites in a copper bowl for puffiness and stability of foam. Fortunately, for most of us who lack a copper bowl, a pinch of <u>cream of tartar</u> achieves the same results. Use in the proportion of <u>1/16 of a teaspoon to one egg white.</u>

Be careful <u>not to overdo the cream of tartar</u> or results will be <u>negative</u>. They will be <u>negative</u> if there's even a <u>touch of yolk</u> in with the whites, and <u>negative</u>, strangely, if beaten in a plastic bowl. <u>Salt</u> increases whipping time and decreases foam's stability, so watch it and don't use any unless you must. <u>Sugar</u> helps the foam not to collapse if added at the <u>right time</u> and in the <u>right amount</u>.

    <u>The time</u>: It should be added <u>gradually after</u> the whites have begun to foam and <u>before</u> they are stiff. When foam stands in peaks, stop! Overbeating is a no-no. Sugar increases stability of foam when baked.

    <u>The amount</u>: <u>2 tablespoons sugar</u> per white for a soft meringue.
               <u>4 tablespoons sugar</u> per white for a hard meringue.
               (Confectioners' sugar preferred but not vital.)

Warning: When beating yolks and whites separately, <u>beat whites first</u>, then no need to wash and dry beater. Whites do not hurt the yolks, improve them in fact, but a touch of yolk or water in whites spells disaster.

When anyone mentioned eggs, my younger brother dearly loved to quote this old-time Limerick:

"A preacher named Henry Ward Beecher
Called a hen a most elegant creature.
The hen, just for that,
Laid an egg in his hat,
And thus did the hen reward Beecher."

Miriam Lusk's    Eggs Foo Yoong

(A good way to enjoy leftover pork.)

leftover pork (chops or roast), chopped
scallions, chopped
bean sprouts
beaten eggs
soy sauce
salt and pepper

Mix in any proportion that suits you. Drop by spoonfuls onto medium-hot greased griddle or skillet. Turn over once. Serve with rice and soy sauce.

Baked Eggs in Maple Toast Cups    (Serves 4 to 6)

3 strips bacon, baked on foil in 325° oven until crisp. Chop and put aside.

1½ tablespoons butter (about)
1½ tablespoons maple syrup

Heat together until butter melts.

6 slices of bread, crusts removed, flattened with a rolling pin, and brushed with butter-syrup mixture. Press each slice into 6 buttered muffin tins, forming a cup. Sprinkle the chopped bacon into each cup.

6 eggs — Break one into each cup.
salt and pepper, to taste, sprinkled on eggs.
Bake in preheated 400° oven for about 15 minutes or until eggs are done to suit you.

If you think bread edges are browning too fast, cover all with foil.

# Creamed Ham and Eggs (serves 6)

A recipe for breakfast, lunch or dinner.
So good, so easy, so consistently overlooked.

1 cup cubed cooked ham
6 hard-boiled eggs, cut up } Prepare and put aside.

¼ cup butter
¼ cup flour } Make a roux by heating butter and mixing in the flour and stirring on heat a minute or so. Remove from heat and add

2 cups milk ever so slowly while stirring constantly. Return to heat and bring to a simmer, stirring for about 2 minutes. Remove from heat and add:

¼ teaspoon dry mustard

¼ teaspoon celery salt

½ teaspoon Worcestershire sauce

salt and pepper, to taste. Now stir your prepared ham and eggs gently into this sauce. It is ready to serve at once, or to hold and reheat in double boiler for later enjoyment.
Serve on toast or toasted English muffins or toasted sandwich buns or corn bread or just as is.

"Nothing helps scenery like ham and eggs."

Mark Twain

# A Poached Egg

In my childhood in New England we always called a poached egg a "dropped egg." By any name it is a delicacy difficult to achieve. First of all the egg must be fresh. Break the egg gently and slide carefully into a cup. From the cup tip it even more gently into a shallow pan of simmering (not boiling!) water about <u>2 inches deep</u>. (The water should contain some vinegar in the proportion of about <u>1 tablespoon vinegar</u> to <u>1 quart water</u>.) Cook for <u>about 4 minutes</u>, coaxing the white up over the yolk with a wooden spoon. White should be firm, the yolk still runny. Remove from water with a <u>slotted spoon</u> and put to rest on a piece of buttered toast on a hot plate. There's no nicer treat in sickness or health, in joy or sorrow. My son prefers a toasted, buttered English muffin. Take your choice.

And speaking of my son, who likes to fool around the kitchen (a graduate of the School of Hotel Administration at Cornell), here's the way he prepares poached eggs for a crowd: He does exactly as indicated above, using a larger skillet so as to hold more eggs. As the eggs reach the perfection stage, he transfers them with a slotted spoon to a bowl of <u>ice water</u>. This stops their cooking and holds them until he sees the whites of the eyes of family and friends assembled at table. Then eggs are carefully returned to simmering <u>salted</u> water this time. (No vinegar the second time around.) About ½ minute in this hot bath does the job. To be truly company prepared, he often does the egg ceremony the night before, removing cooked eggs from ice water to platter, covering with plastic and refrigerating overnight. This all sounds woefully complicated, but those who have conquered the art seem to glory in it.

# Light and Lovely Baked Omelet (serves 4)

4 eggs, at room temperature, separated into two bowls.
Beat the whites into stiff peaks first.
To the yolks add:

3 tablespoons hot water ⎱ Beat the yolks until a bit thick
½ teaspoon salt ⎰ and pale, using the same beater.
- - - - (The egg white left on beater an
advantage. Reverse order a disaster.)

Now fold the whites, gently, into the yolks
and turn into a heavy 10-inch frying pan
in which you have heated

1 tablespoon butter (about) until it froths, but not browns.

Tilt the butter around to cover bottom and
sides of pan before pouring in the eggs. Bake
in preheated 350° oven for 15 minutes
or so, or until slightly tanned and a
little firm when touched with finger.
Serve at once. Cut into pie-like pieces, or
just scoop with a spoon.

To this basic, delicate omelet, if you are so inclined,
you may add to the beaten yolks (before folding in
the whites) one or several of the following:
pepper, grated Parmesan, grated Cheddar,
chopped parsley, chives, chervil, grated onion,
chopped ham, chopped cooked bacon, sautéed mushrooms.
Use any amounts, to taste, but go lightly.

# Herbed Potato Omelet   (serves 4)

Excellent breakfast or late supper dish, especially when served with hot corn bread.

1½ cups diced raw potatoes — Cook in slightly salted water until tender. Drain well.

4 eggs, beaten

½ teaspoon dried basil, more if fresh

½ teaspoon dried oregano, more if fresh

½ teaspoon salt

3 tablespoons green pepper, chopped fine

3 Tablespoons scallions, chopped fine

Mix together well, and then stir in the cooked potatoes.

2 tablespoons corn oil, heated in good-sized skillet.

When oil is hot, pour in the omelet mixture and cook, uncovered, over fairly low heat until nicely browned on the bottom. Do not stir at any time and do not hurry it. 15 minutes is about the time it takes. Loosen around edges and under omelet with spatula before inverting onto warm platter. Or serve sections directly from pan onto individual plates, brown side up.

Sidney Nisbet's **Blender Quiche** ～ Serves 4 to 6 people.
(Oh so easy! Makes its own crust. Excellent for brunch or Sunday supper.)

(1.) ～ 10 slices of bacon, placed on a cookie sheet that has sides. Bake in 350° oven
(you may substitute    until crisp. Place cooked bacon on paper towels to absorb
1 cup chopped,    fat. Crumble bacon and set aside.
cooked ham for bacon.)

(2) ～ 1 large onion, coarsely chopped and sautéed gently in a bit of butter.

(3) ～ 1 cup shredded cheese ～ sharp Cheddar or Swiss or Gruyère. (About 4 ounces)

(4.) ～ 3 large eggs (or 4 small) ⎫ Place in blender or food processor.
1½ cups milk ⎪ Blend thoroughly and pour into
¾ cup Bisquick ⎪ well-buttered, normal-sized Pyrex or
2 tablespoons prepared mustard* ⎬ Corningware pie plate. Sprinkle the
⎪ prepared bacon, onion and cheese
¼ teaspoon nutmeg ⎪ thereon. Help them to submerge. Bake in
pinch cayenne pepper ⎪ preheated 350 oven for 45 minutes.
black pepper, freshly ground, to taste ⎭ Cool about 10 minutes before serving
in pie-like wedges.

### Blender Quiche Variations

Spinach Quiche ～ Use 1 cup chopped, cooked spinach in place of bacon or ham.

Mushroom Quiche ～ Sauté 1 cup sliced mushrooms with the onions.

Chicken Quiche ～ Substitute chicken for bacon or ham.

Eggplant and Tomato Quiche ～ Place one whole, small eggplant on
greased pie plate in 350° oven. Bake about 45 minutes. Cool, peel, chop.
To the eggplant add 2 tomatoes, peeled and chopped, and drain
all thoroughly in a colander or strainer. Add eggplant and tomato
to sautéed onion and cook about 2 minutes more. In step ＊ 4
(the blender) omit the mustard and nutmeg and add 1 clove garlic
and ½ teaspoon oregano. Substitute ½ cup grated Parmesan
cheese rather than other cheeses mentioned. No meat used in
this. Better add ½ teaspoon salt.

Dream up your own variations! Possibilities are limitless.

＊ Sidney uses 2 tablespoons Durkee's "Famous Sauce" + ½ teaspoon dry mustard.

# About Cheese

"Cheese — milk's leap toward immortality."

In England in the early 18ᵗʰ century the making of Cheddar cheese was well established. It was named for the town in which it was made and was a cooperative venture in that it used the milk from all the cows in the region mixed together. Defoe is reported to have said, "By this method the goodness of the cheese is preserved, and without all dispute, it is the best cheese that England affords, if not, that the whole world affords." Amen, say I, as is apparent by the number of times it's called for in this book. I'm never without a Cheddar-type cheese. In New England we used to call it "rat trap cheese". Too good for rats, believe me. My father was forever saying, "Apple pie without cheese is like a kiss without a squeeze." There seem to be young people who have never heard that once overused quotation, nor tasted the haunting combination that inspired it.

It is mostly true that briefly aged cheese was staple food for the poor and sometimes called "white meat." The rich chose well-aged cheese such as Roquefort and Brie, and served it at the end of a meal as a digestive. It is claimed that the ancient Greeks ate cheese at the end of a meal also, for the purpose of inducing thirst for more wine. Cheese, like wine, can be a life's study.

My grandfather used to pontificate that

there were never less than six kinds of cheese on his table to round off a meal. Heavens. I might add that he was well rounded, in the days when that was the fashion. It didn't kill him either. He lived to a ripe old age.

I serve cheese for dessert as an accompaniment to fruit only and never when cheese is served with cocktails at the beginning of a meal. The Edwardians did not serve cocktails nor were they diet-minded as we are. "Too much of a good thing" did not seem to enter their consciousness. To be a trencherman was a matter of pride.

~~~~~~~~~

Brillat-Savarin spoke for his era when he said, "A dinner that ends without cheese is like a beautiful woman with only one eye."

~~~~~~~~~

There is a great amount of cheese used in various dishes throughout this book, but they all seem to fall under different categories such as Appetizers, Bird~Beast~Fish, and Greens~Grains~Vegetables. Hence, only three lonely recipes end up in the Cheese section that follows.

~~~~~~~~~

# Easy Rarebit  (Serves 2)

One (10½ ounce) can cream of mushroom soup ⎫ Stir together in saucepan.
½ cup milk ⎬ Bring to boil, stirring often,
　　　　　　　　　　　　　　　　　　⎭ then add :

1 cup sharp grated Cheddar, pressed down, and
½ teaspoon Worcestershire sauce

　　　　　　Heat just until cheese melts, stirring.
　　　　　　Serve at once, pouring into two plates!
paprika to garnish rarebit.
melba toast, in triangles, framing the rarebit.

# Cheese Pudding  (Serves 4)

1 cup soft bread crumbs, soaked in
1 cup milk ⌁ Then add the following :
1 cup shredded sharp Cheddar
2 tablespoons melted butter
salt and cayenne pepper, to taste

　　　　　　Pour into buttered, one-quart baking dish.
　　　　　　Hold as long as you want. When ready to
　　　　　　dine, bake in preheated 350° oven for
　　　　　　30 to 35 minutes.
Serve for breakfast, luncheon, or supper.

Both recipes on this page are emergency numbers that
can be concocted in minutes.

# Tomato Cheese Soufflé (serves 4)

1 cup tomato juice
3 Tablespoons quick-cooking tapioca
} Boil together for 1 minute, stirring constantly. Then stir in:

1 cup grated Cheddar cheese
½ teaspoon salt
dash of cayenne pepper
1 tablespoon butter
} Stir until cheese is melted. Remove from heat and cool slightly.

3 eggs — Separate them, beating the whites stiff first* then the yolks.
} Stir well-beaten yolks into above. Fold the whites in fast.

Turn into a buttered soufflé dish and place in pan of hot water. Bake in 350° oven about 50 minutes, or until firm to touch.

~~~~~~~

I've often said that soufflés are not recommended for a company meal. This one is different. It holds up nobly. Bacon and corn bread or muffins or corn sticks make happy accompaniments. Acceptable as breakfast, lunch or supper dish.

~~~~~~~

* See About Eggs (page 126) if you want to know why whites are best beaten first.

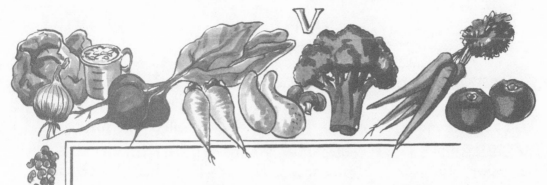

# V

## Greens ~ Grains ~ Vegetables

# Basic French Dressing

¼ cup vinegar
½ cup vegetable oil
    (I use corn oil)
1 teaspoon sugar
½ teaspoon salt
½ teaspoon garlic salt
½ teaspoon dry mustard
¼ teaspoon paprika
⅛ teaspoon pepper

Measure all ingredients into a glass jar with cover. Shake vigorously to mix. Keep in refrigerator. A fine dressing as is, or you may add crumbled Roquefort or blue cheese, or chopped herbs in season, or chili sauce and a bit of mayonnaise, or some horseradish. Make your own variations.

Here is a dressing no home should be without:

### Hidden Valley Original Ranch Salad Dressing Mix

It is in every market everywhere and has to be the best tasting dressing in the world. Directions are on the green package. I make it with fat-free milk, often stretching it with generous amounts of cottage cheese.

# Poppy Seed Dressing

1 medium onion, roughly cut up
1 teaspoon salt
2 teaspoons dry mustard
⅔ cup sugar
⅔ cup vinegar

Blend in blender.

1 cup corn oil, added slowly to blender. When well incorporated pour dressing into glass jar with cover. Then stir in:
3 tablespoons poppy seeds (seeds are best if toasted.)

Poppy Seed Dressing is especially good with salads
composed of the following:

① avocado and grapefruit
② tomato and white grapes
③ sweet onion rings and mandarin orange sections
④ pear halves filled with cottage cheese and chopped scallions

Arrange on
lettuce leaves.
(Boston is best, or
so I think.)

~~~~~~~~~

## Pennsylvania Dutch Hot Dressing (serves 4 to 6)

This is for "wilting" greens: dandelion, curly endive or escarole.
It provides a salad and vegetable all in one. A rare old-time treat.

2 eggs
¼ cup sugar
¼ cup vinegar
1 cup water
½ teaspoon dry mustard
½ teaspoon salt
1 tablespoon flour

When greens and bacon, below, are
prepared, toss all this into blender in
order given. Blend well. Pour into
saucepan and, when ready to serve, bring
just to a boil, no more. Pour over
prepared greens. Add the bacon.
Toss well and serve at once in sauce
dishes or bowls.

↓

1 quart greens, washed, coarsely cut up, pressed down.
6 slices bacon, cut small with scissors
        and baked or fried until
    crisp. Drain off fat and put bacon on paper towels.

Have this all
ready before
making dressing!

~~~~~~~~~

## Cole Slaw Dressing (the best) (for 1 quart shredded cabbage)

1 small can evaporated milk
½ teaspoon salt
¼ teaspoon pepper
4 tablespoons sugar
4 tablespoons vinegar

Stir this all together in glass jar with
cover. Keep refrigerated until ready to
mix into finely shredded cabbage. You
may augment cabbage with chopped celery or
green onions or green peppers or shredded
carrots — any one or all.
You may substitute maple syrup or honey for sugar.

~~~~~~~~~

140

George Sawyer's   Creamy Roquefort Dressing

¼ pound Roquefort or good blue cheese

1 cup sour cream

¼ cup mayonnaise

¼ cup sherry

¼ cup vinegar (wine preferred
           but regular cider vinegar O.K.)

1 tablespoon grated onion

½ teaspoon salt

½ teaspoon garlic salt

¼ teaspoon paprika

Coarsely crumble cheese into bowl. Add remaining ingredients, stirring until well blended. Cover, refrigerate at least one hour.

George is my nephew, a great cook and judge of good food. His remark when he sent me this recipe was: "Super on hearts of lettuce. I just ate a whole head." He calls this recipe "really outstanding." So do I.

Jean Tyson's     <u>Apple Slaw</u>   (serves 6)

      When Jean and her family head for the Tyson family farm in South Strafford, Vermont, for Thanksgiving each year (one of those "over the river and through the woods to Grandmother's house we go" events), it is traditional for her to bring this Apple Slaw. Try it, you'll love it. The recipe is easily multiplied.

<u>2 red-skinned apples</u>, not peeled, just <u>cored</u> and <u>diced</u>     } Tossed together in bowl large enough for whole recipe. (Lemon prevents apple browning as well as adding flavor!)

<u>1 Tablespoon lemon juice</u>

<u>3 cups shredded cabbage</u>, added to above apples.

<u>1 tablespoon honey</u>
<u>½ cup sour cream</u> (about)
<u>salt and pepper</u>, to taste     } Stir together and spoon over apple-cabbage mixture. Toss lightly.

      Chill before serving.

## Ever-Ready Cole Slaw (Serves a gang, keeps indefinitely, is fat free.)

1 large head cabbage
2 big carrots
celery stalks, several          } Grind. Here's hoping you
1 big onion                          have a food processor to
1 red pepper                        do the job.
1 green pepper

1 gallon of water (4 quarts) } Mix and soak the above in this
1 tablespoon salt                  solution overnight. Drain well
                                         in the morning and then add
                                         the following mixture:

1 cup regular cider vinegar
1 cup water                        } Combine and stir into
1 cup sugar                          cabbage mixture.
1 tablespoon celery seed        Refrigerate. Keeps and keeps
1 tablespoon mustard seed    and is very special.

Once upon a time I cheated and skipped the soaking
process. The results were fine. (I used 1 teaspoon salt
in the vinegar mixture.)

# Jellied Cucumber Salad (serves 6)

1 tablespoon unflavored gelatin, soaked in
2 tablespoons lemon juice for about 5 minutes.
3/4 cup chicken broth, brought to boil and poured over
      soaked gelatin. Stir until thoroughly dissolved
      and add:

2 cups grated cucumber (peeled and seeded before grating)
1 tablespoon sugar
1 tablespoon grated onion
1/2 teaspoon dill weed
      (more if fresh)
1/4 teaspoon paprika
a dash of green coloring
salt to taste

Mix and spoon into oiled individual molds or small cups.

Chill. Unmold onto slices of tomato and garnish with a dab of mayonnaise topped with a dusting of dill (or better still, a sprig of fresh dill). Serve on lettuce or not, as you wish.

~~~~~~~~~~

# Maple Waldorf Salad (serves 6)

3 cups apples, cubed, with or without skins, placed in bowl.
1 tablespoon lemon juice
2 tablespoons mayonnaise
2 tablespoons maple syrup
1/2 cup chopped walnuts
3/4 cup raisins

Mixed and stirred into apples at once so they don't darken. Then add:

Chill and serve on lettuce. You may want to pass extra mayonnaise.

~~~~~~~~~~

Sarah Gridle's     Guacamole  ⌐ Texas style
(A salad or a dip)
(Serves 4 or more)

2 large, ripe avocados, peeled, mashed
          with a fork ("Don't blend into a
          mush", says Sarah.)
3 tablespoons lemon juice
1 small onion, chopped fine
1 small green chili pepper, chopped (optional)
⅛ teaspoon ground coriander
½ teaspoon salt
1 clove garlic, minced
3 tablespoons mayonnaise
1 tomato, peeled, seeded, chopped
1 teaspoon Worcestershire
cayenne pepper, a dash

Mix all together,
leaving avocado
pit in the mixture
to keep it from
turning dark.
Cover and chill
until ready to serve.
Remove pit.
Surround with tomato slices
on leaves of lettuce or not.
Arrange on platter for
self-service or on individual
salad plates.

This may be served as an appetizer dip with
tortilla chips.  Bite-sized pieces of cauliflower
are especially good with this dip also.

# Homestead Salad  (serves 8)
(Kindness of Dorothy Fox)

½ cup sugar
1 heaping tablespoon flour          } Mix thoroughly in
1 heaping tablespoon prepared mustard ) small saucepan.

½ cup regular cider vinegar stirred into above. Cook,
    stirring constantly until smooth,
    thickened, clarified. Allow to cool
    somewhat as you prepare the following:

1 ten-ounce package frozen mixed vegetables brought to a
    boil in very little slightly salted water.
    Boil 2 minutes, tip into strainer and
    shower with cold water.

1 fifteen-ounce can kidney beans, drained and rinsed
    in strainer

1 cup chopped celery

½ cup chopped green pepper

¼ cup onion, chopped fine (Bermuda, red Spanish, or scallions)

    Having placed the five above ingredients
in adequate-sized container, pour the sauce over all.
Mix well and add salt to taste. Cover and refrigerate
for 24 hours. This can take the place of vegetable and
salad. Delicious and different and fat-free. Especially
tempting served in chilled sauce dishes. Keeps for ages.

# Old-Fashioned Macaroni Salad (serves 6)

2 cups elbow macaroni — Cook according to package directions. Drain, chill.

6 hard-boiled eggs, chopped
1 cup chopped celery
green onions, finely chopped
      (about 2 generous tablespoons)
3 ounces sharp Cheddar, cubed
3/4 to 1 cup mayonnaise
1/2 teaspoon dry mustard
      (rubbed between fingers
       for lump-free spreading)
1/4 teaspoon salt

Mix together in bowl. Then stir in the chilled macaroni.

This may be done way ahead of serving.

Serve on a bed of

shredded lettuce   and garnish with

toasted slivered almonds

Try serving this with Garden Tomato Soup (page 66) and crusty French bread or Melba Toast (page 27) and sweet butter, for a simple luncheon that is simply delicious.

Macaroni salad, like potato salad, has many variations. One or all of the following things may be added to above salad according to your taste: chopped parsley, green pepper, pimiento, black olives, freshly ground pepper, a dash of vinegar. Also you may substitute any pasta you desire in place of the elbow macaroni.

# Potato Salad (serves 8)

4 Idaho potatoes, preferred but not vital. (You want about 4 cups of cubed potatoes.)

① Boil, unpeeled. Chill overnight. Peel and cube next day or

② Peel and cube raw. Boil in salted water until just tender. Drain and save water for bread or soup. This makes a less starchy salad or

③ Boil new potatoes with skins on and dice, skin and all, when cool.

Place prepared, diced potatoes in glass or ceramic bowl of size to contain whole recipe.

1 or 2 bunches of scallions (or 1 medium onion), chopped fine

2 teaspoons dried dill, or 2 tablespoons chopped fresh

¼ cup chopped fresh parsley

1 small green pepper, chopped fine

½ cup chopped celery

4 hard-boiled eggs ~ Cut up 3. Save 1 for garnish.

Add this to cubed potatoes.

1 tablespoon sugar

3 tablespoons vinegar

3 tablespoons oil (optional)

salt and pepper, to taste

½ cup mayonnaise

½ cup sour cream or yogurt

About: You judge.

Mix this together thoroughly before pouring over all of above. Toss salad gently. Avoid making it into a mush. Chill salad for several hours to blend flavors. Overnight is best. Serve on a bed of lettuce, garnishing the mound of potato salad with the reserved egg and some paprika. Sliced tomatoes, cucumbers, and radish roses may be added for decoration as well as taste. I have a friend who tops the salad with crumbled, crisp bacon. Delicious but decidedly optional.

## Molded Pineapple Salad* (serves 6)

1 package (3 ounces) lemon gelatin, poured into a bowl.

1 cup boiling water, poured over gelatin and stirred until gelatin is completely dissolved. Then add all of the following, stirring in well:

½ cup cold water

⅛ teaspoon salt

½ cup shredded carrots

1 can (8 ounces) crushed pineapple (unsweetened) Do not drain.

Let refrigerate until slightly thickened. Stir well so as to have ingredients in proper suspension. Then spoon into oiled (not buttered) individual molds(6) or a one-quart mold. Chill until set. Unmold and serve on lettuce. Top with mayonnaise.

## Favorite Tomato Aspic (serves 6)

1 package (3 ounces) lemon gelatin, poured into a bowl.

1 ¼ cups boiling water, poured over gelatin and stirred until gelatin completely dissolved. Then add following:

1 can (8 ounces) tomato sauce

1½ tablespoons vinegar

½ teaspoon salt

1 teaspoon onion juice

dash of Tabasco

ground cloves, just a sprinkle

2 cups chopped celery

When this is all stirred together, refrigerate, and follow directions exactly as with Molded Pineapple Salad above.

* I served this salad, one time, to a woman whose husband had been called away on business, so couldn't join us. On his return home he asked his wife what my dinner had consisted of. When she came to the Molded Pineapple Salad he said, "I'm glad I missed it." "But why?" said she. He replied, "That mouldy salad must have been awful."

# Polly Cox's   Surprise Salad   (Serves 8)

1 one-pound can sweetened gooseberries, drained, liquid reserved
and water added to equal 1¾ cups.
Bring syrup to boil.

2 small packages Lemon Jell-O
(or Royal brand)     Dissolve in above hot syrup.
½ cup sugar

2 cups orange juice, added to above dissolved Jell-O.
Chill until partially set.

2 cups thinly sliced celery  )  Fold into slightly jellied
1 cup broken walnuts  )  mixture above — along
with the gooseberries.

Pour into mold of your choice.
(I use 6" x 10" baking dish.)

This salad is deliciously different. The surprise
is the main ingredient, which guests can
rarely identify.

## Zucchini and Grapefruit Salad
This is different — and so's the dressing.

tender young zucchini, washed, not peeled, cut into thin
circles and then into the finest julienne strips.
grapefruit, prepare whole sections free of all membrane.
Or, if this is too much like work, cut grapefruit
in half and dig out sections with a serrated spoon.
Whatever you do, drain the grapefruit on paper towels
so salad won't be watery. One whole grapefruit is
sufficient for 4 salads (unless you're making salad the main dish).
Arrange little mounds of zucchini on lettuce and surround with
the grapefruit.
Here's the recipe for the dressing, which is better passed at the table
for self-service:

### Raspberry Dressing (serves 6 or 8)
½ cup raspberry jam
2 tablespoons prepared mustard ⎫ Mix together
1 tablespoon honey          ⎬ thoroughly.
                            ⎭ Then stir in

6 tablespoons vinegar and
½ cup vegetable oil, added slowly while stirring
                                      vigorously.

People will take a small serving the first time around.
Then watch them come back for lots more.

This dressing goes well with a pear and sweet onion salad.
Also with an apple and onion salad. (But be sure to hold
apple slices in lemon water until almost ready to serve so
apples don't turn brown. And dry them with paper towels.)

Elise's  Barley Casserole  (serves 8)

½ cup butter (¼ pound), heated in large skillet.

2 generous onions, coarsely chopped and stirred into butter. Cook gently about 5 minutes.

¾ pound fresh mushrooms, cleaned, trimmed, sliced and cooked with onions another 5 minutes.

1½ cups pearl barley
(not the quick-cooking variety)  Add barley to onions and mushrooms and cook and stir for 5 or 10 minutes until barley is light brown.

3 cups chicken or beef broth, poured into above and stirred about to pick up browned juices. Then stir in the following:

1 teaspoon salt

⅛ teaspoon cayenne pepper

½ cup chopped fresh parsley

Transfer this completed skillet mixture to a 2 quart, buttered casserole. Cover.  Bake in preheated 350° oven for about 1½ hours or until barley is tender and liquid is absorbed.

Barley has sustained the human race for eons.
A welcome substitute for potatoes.
This casserole may be prepared ahead, then baked just before serving.  Goes beautifully with any barbecued meat — especially a boned and butterflied leg of lamb.

# Plain Boiled Rice (Serves 4)

The chief food of half the world's population.
There are 2500 different varieties!
Buy the best long-grain Carolina rice.

<u>2 cups water</u>, brought to boil in large, heavy saucepan.
Add to the boiling water:
<u>1 tablespoon butter</u>
<u>3/4 teaspoon salt</u>
<u>1 cup rice</u>, stirred into above. Cover, simmer on <u>very low heat</u>
for 20 minutes. Don't peek. That's it. Fluff with fork.

## Brown Rice (serves 4)

Do exactly as directed above, but cook for <u>50 minutes</u>, possibly more.
Better check to see if it needs more water during cooking.
(Brown rice sometimes needs washing before cooking. Wash in strainer
under running water.)

## Perfect Wild Rice (serves 4)

Wild rice is a native of North America and only a distant cousin of
Asian rice. It contains more protein than other rice and is rich
in lysine, which regular rice lacks.
<u>1 cup wild rice</u>, washed thoroughly in strainer. Put rice in container
in which you plan to cook it — a large one. Pour <u>boiling
water</u> over rice, cover, let stand all night. Next day
drain off any excess water. Then cover with <u>cold water</u>
and add
<u>3/4 teaspoon salt</u> Bring to boil, cover, and simmer <u>1 hour</u>.

(Check for need of more water during simmering.) Drain cooked rice in strainer or colander and rinse with cold water. Rice is then transferred to double boiler. Test for saltiness and add a generous dollop of butter. Rice is ready to heat when you are ready to eat.

Plain boiled white or brown rice, as presented on previous page, has its very special place. But it may also be enhanced in many ways after cooking — by the addition of canned pineapple chunks (my favorite way), sautéed mushrooms and onions, toasted slivered almonds, raisins or currants or pine nuts. To be company-ready, I often prepare rice in the morning and 'reheat' in a colander over boiling water when it's almost time to serve.

## Baked Rice and Cheese (serves 4)

Leftover rice (white, brown or wild)? Here's your dish.

4 tablespoons butter, melted
4 tablespoons flour
2 cups milk
½ teaspoon salt
pepper, to taste

> Make this into a white sauce (page 162). Season with:

½ teaspoon Worcestershire Sauce
sprinkle of thyme (generous)
2 cups cooked rice
1 cup grated Cheddar cheese

> Spread half of rice in bottom of buttered casserole. Then add half of sauce, then half of cheese. Repeat. Top with:

¼ cup buttered crumbs

Bake, uncovered, in 350° oven for about 20 minutes.

154

## Rice-Vegetable Casserole (serves 8 or more)

The perfect one-dish accompaniment to any barbecued bird, beast or fish. A summer favorite.

1 large onion, sliced thin, separated into rings

1 medium eggplant, peeled and cubed

1 cup uncooked rice
(long-grain Carolina preferable)

1 green pepper, cut small

3 small summer squash, yellow, sliced

3 tomatoes, scalded to loosen skins, peeled, sliced very thin

Salt and pepper, to taste

Using half of each prepared vegetable, layer them in the order listed in a large, buttered casserole with cover. Salt and pepper each layer according to taste. Repeat layers, ending with tomatoes which should cover all and impart their juices to the rice.

1 can (10½ ounces) Campbell's Consommé

¼ pound butter

Heat together until butter melts. Stir and spoon over vegetables, stir and spoon, until all used up and every bit of surface is anointed.

Bake, covered, in preheated 350° oven for a good 30 minutes. Remove cover and bake another 15 minutes, or until liquid is absorbed.

# Almond Herb Pilaf (Serves 4 to 6)

1 tablespoon butter, heated in pan large enough for whole recipe.

1 medium onion, chopped ⎫
1 clove garlic, minced ⎭ Heat in the butter until softened only.

1 cup long-grain raw rice, stirred into above for about one minute.

2 cups beef broth (one 10½ ounce can with ⎫  Stir into above. Bring to
      sufficient water added to make 2 cups ) ⎪  boil, then simmer,
1 teaspoon dried marjoram (or 3 of fresh chopped) ⎬ covered, about 20 minutes
1 teaspoon dried basil (or 3 of fresh chopped) ⎪  or until rice is cooked and all
½ teaspoon salt    — — — — — — — — — — ⎭ liquid absorbed. Remove from
                                           heat. Let stand, covered,
                                           5 minutes. Then stir in:

¾ cup toasted slivered almonds*
           Serve with pride.

Pilaf may be reheated in strainer over boiling water if you prefer to prepare ahead.

        This is a sufficiently flavorful dish so that plain meat and plain vegetable with it is recommended. Let them be mildly seasoned in the interest of contrast: broiled lamb chop or chicken or fish, for example; and a creamed vegetable, again for contrast, as everything else is somewhat dry. The night I first tried this rice dish I had a few fresh peas, so barely cooked them, chopped up some celery, did not cook it so it could supply crunch, and immersed the peas and celery in a simple white sauce (page 162). It proved a highly successful meal.

*To toast almonds: Spread in shallow pan. Bake at 300° about 15 minutes or until vaguely tanned. The improved flavor is worth the effort.

Ginger's    Tomato Sauce

( To go with pasta or Black Beans or Pita Pizza, which follows.)

1 can Progresso peeled tomatoes (1 pound and 12 ounces)   Simmer until
                    Chop and put in cookpot, enamelware   reduced and
                    is best.  Add:                        saucelike, without a
                                                          cover. This takes
Thyme , a pinch                                           about ½ hour. Stir
2 cloves garlic, minced                                   often. When cooked
1 tablespoon dried oregano                                add:

3 tablespoons vegetable oil of your choice.  It is now finished for those
                    of vegetarian persuasion. For those who prefer
                    meat; take
1 pound groundchuck and put in hot salted skillet. Separate
                    well and brown nicely. Pour off any fat
                    and pat also with paper towels to remove
                    more fat. Mix into the tomato sauce
                    and the dish is ready for various uses.


Ginger's    Pita Pizza   (Plan 1 or 2 small pita halves
                                        per person. )

( Ginger claims all kids love this, and not only kids. )

Buy small pitas (about 6" diameter). Split and bake
in 350° oven until crisp but not brown. Remove
from oven and paint the rough side with the
vegetable oil of your choice.

Now spread the pita halves with Ginger's Tomato Sauce
(preceeding page), as thick or thin as you want and
with or without the inclusion of meat. Garnish with
the following:

sliced mushrooms ⎫
onion rings      ⎬ optional, but oh-so-good
grated mozzarella cheese and
grated Parmesan cheese

oregano, a tiny sprinkle if you like.

This whole operation, from start to finish, should take place on
a foil-covered cookie sheet. Slide the pita pizzas into a
preheated 450° oven and bake until cheese bubbles.
Careful, they cook fast.

~~~~~~~~~~~

Ginger's   Black Beans   (serves 8 or more)

1 one-pound bag black turtle beans, washed ever so carefully and
soaked overnight in kettle in which you plan to
cook them, in more than enough water to cover.
(They soak up a lot of water.) In the morning
(without draining) add:

1 medium onion, cut up
3 cloves garlic, crushed
rosemary, a pinch
thyme, a pinch
1 bay leaf
parsley, a few sprigs
4 whole cloves
3 Tablespoons soy sauce
water to cover (or some stock if you have it)

Simmer a good 4 hours, adding water as needed, and stirring. Keep covered. Be careful not to scorch. This may be served as is, or with rice, white or brown. But it is best mixed with Ginger's Tomato Sauce (with the meat added). A health food dish (with rice and a green salad) that could cause you to go out and lick your weight in wildcats.

# Southern Spoon Bread   (serves 6)

1 cup yellow corn meal, put in good-sized saucepan.
2 cups cold water, stirred into corn meal thoroughly.
1 teaspoon salt, added to corn meal and water mixture.
> Heat and stir until mixture comes to boil and
> is smooth and thick. Remove from stove
> and add:

2 tablespoons butter, stirred into meal until melted.
> Then add

1 cup milk and

4 eggs That have been well beaten and

1 cup grated sharp Cheddar cheese, pressed down.

> Stir all together well and then pour
> into buttered 1½ quart soufflé dish
> or baking dish and bake in preheated
> 400° oven for 40 minutes. Turn off
> heat and leave in oven another 5 minutes
> or so.

This goes especially well with ham or pork.
If you want a bland, more traditional spoon bread, omit cheese.
(But, to me, its better with the cheese.)

Here's a menu in which I like to include Spoon Bread:

Ham Loaf Caramel (page 100)

Southern Spoon Bread

Boiled Fresh Spinach
garnished with hard-boiled
egg slices. (Pass the vinegar
cruet.)

Molded Pineapple Salad (page 148)

Pear Melba (page 260)

good color scheme, good eating.

Jean Rowlands' __Spoon Bread__ (serves 4)

1 cup yellow cornmeal (stone ground if possible) Place all this in a saucepan and stir over heat until it comes to a boil. Remove from heat and stir until you are sure there are no lumps. Forget it for 5 or 10 minutes so that it cools a bit. Then add:

1 teaspoon salt

2 cups cold water

1 cup milk

3 unbeaten eggs and stir them in enthusiastically.
Now place:

3 tablespoons butter in a baking dish of proper size to hold whole recipe. Put dish into preheated 475° oven until butter bubbles but does not brown (about 5 minutes).

Into the hot butter plop the corn mixture and bake about 45 minutes on middle shelf of this 475° oven. It puffs and acquires a heavenly brown crust. Watch it toward the last so as not to let it get too brown. Unless served instantly it deflates a bit, but no harm. You'll wonder how anything so good can be so easy.

Jean says she sometimes serves this Spoon Bread for breakfast with sausage, or for lunch with a salad. Served for dinner I like it with ham and Farmer's Cabbage (page 172) and a salad that lends a note of sweetness (maybe a Maple Waldorf salad (page 143).

# Favorite Ways of Cooking Various Vegetables

For serving a few people, I like to use this handy grater on the medium side as pictured. Set on a piece of waxed paper and grate vegetable of your choice. (For many servings a food processor proves a boon.) Heat butter in a pan and, when its just hot enough to cause a sizzle but butter is not browned, slide the grated vegetable from paper into pan. Stir over high heat a minute or two, no more. Remove from heat, clamp on lid and allow to steam in its own juices about 5 minutes. Salt and pepper to taste, serve. Thats it.

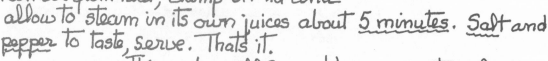

      This works well for cabbage, carrots, celery (Chop rather than grate celery and season with a touch of celery seed), onions, parsnips (a touch of brown sugar added), summer squash, turnips, zucchini.

      Another approach, especially if one must avoid fats, is to cut above vegetables into small pieces (but not necessarily to grate them), add a small amount of water, a bouillon cube (or granules) in chicken or beef flavor. Bring quickly to a boil, stirring once to distribute the bouillon flavor, and cook just long enough for crisp tenderness but not mushiness. Its best if all water is boiled away but if not, serve in its juices with slotted spoon. Its amazing how much a touch of bouillon can do flavorwise.

And the butter is not missed. (Of course it's better with butter. What isn't? This is only to tell you how to avoid its use if that is necessary healthwise.)

~~~~~~~~~~

Another treatment for sparingly cooked vegetables that are still watery is to make a sauce of what too many drain off into the sink. Pour off vegetable water into a measuring cup. In the proportion of ⅓ cup fluid to 1 teaspoon cornstarch (or 1 cup fluid to 1 tablespoon cornstarch), mix well and pour back on vegetables. Stir over heat until thickened and shiny. This only takes seconds and adds much to attractiveness, taste, nutrition, and cohesiveness. (The latter characteristic making them stay put nicely if serving a plate dinner.)

~~~~~~~~~~

If one is on a salt-free diet, the bouillon treatment (on page 160 ) won't do. Then is the time to fall back mostly on 'herbs. Here's a list of vegetables with suggested happy seasoning companions. Low-salt food need not be boring and is popular these days whether doctor-directed or not. (See page 164 )

Not counting salt and butter, the greatest seasonings, to me, are LEMONS, the juice and grated rind.
(Forget plastic lemons and ReaLemon in a bottle.)
and ONIONS and their whole family of garlic, scallions, leeks, chives, shallots.
(Remember the Biblical Israelites were about to forget the Promised Land because of lack of onions en route to that destination. No wonder.)

162

# Sauces for Cooked Vegetables

The greatest way to stretch and often to enhance cooked vegetables is to put them in a Cream or White Sauce. (Titles are interchangeable.) It's smart to use this technique when other parts of the main course are on the dry side, and especially when no gravy is served.

## White Sauce (serves 2. May be multiplied endlessly.)

2 tablespoons butter, melted in saucepan

2 tablespoons flour, stirred into butter and cooked and stirred
<br>This is → until flour loses its raw taste but is not browned.
<br>a roux → Remove from heat. This is crucial.

1 cup milk, added gradually to roux while stirring constantly. When well mixed and lump free, return to heat and stir until thickened and smooth. Careful not to scorch!

Salt and pepper, to taste
<br>This has to be the most basic of all basics in cooking.

The fundamental sauce above is the progenitor of innumerable sauces. To name a few:

Cheese Sauce — Add about ½ cup cubed sharp cheese or grated Parmesan. Heat in double boiler until cheese melts.

Mornay Sauce — Add a combination of Swiss and Parmesan cheese. Just before serving, stir in a beaten egg yolk and some more butter.

Béchamel Sauce — Use half good strong Chicken Stock and half milk (or cream) in place of all milk.

Curry Sauce — add curry to taste and touch of ground ginger.

# Dr. Jordan's White Sauce

(Famed doctor of the Lahey Clinic who was a genius at putting delicate digestions back in order.)

1 cup milk
2 tablespoons flour } Whirled in blender, then transferred to saucepan or double boiler and stirred over heat until thickened. Then add:
salt, pepper, butter.

Dr. Jordan claimed the roux method on previous page to be indigestible for frail constitutions.

To go even further, health wise, leave out the butter for a fat-free sauce. Substitute a bouillon cube for flavor. (Eliminating salt and pepper) Its' amazingly good and a boon to those who are cholesterol conscious.

~~~~~~~~~~

Plain White Sauce can be doctored up endlessly, depending on how it is used and your particular taste buds. Aside from cheese and bouillon cubes there is paprika, all the onion family, horseradish, Tabasco, and an imposing array of herbs. (page 164) Cream may be substituted for milk. Elegant.

~~~~~~~~~~

# Cream Cheese Sauce

½ cup milk
1 eight-ounce package Cream Cheese } Cook together over very low heat. Stir until smooth. Then stir in what follows.
¼ cup grated Parmesan cheese

½ teaspoon onion salt

chopped parsley and/or pimiento (optional, for color)

Serve over any cooked vegetable of your choice. Cream Cheese is not rich, as its name sounds, yet satisfies one's longing for what seems sinful.

~~~~~~~~~~

## Seasoning Suggestions for Vegetables

**Asparagus** ~ lemon juice / mustard / nutmeg

**Artichokes** ~ Put 4 or 5 coriander seeds in cooking water.

**Avocado** ~ onion / garlic / saffron / lime juice / pepper / dill

**Beans (String)** ~ savory (the bean herb) / chervil / dill / marjoram / rosemary

**Beans (Lima)** ~ garlic / allspice / lemon zest / chili powder

**Beets** ~ vinegar / pepper / horseradish / chives / onion / cloves / caraway / bay leaf

**Broccoli** ~ oregano / horseradish / scallions / lemon juice / pepper / parsley / chives

**Cabbage** ~ onion / dill / parsley / pepper / celery seed / oregano / paprika / savory

**Carrots** ~ onion / ginger / parsley / pepper

**Cauliflower** ~ onion / pimiento / toasted almonds

**Celery** ~ basil / celery seed / scallions / pepper / green pepper / garlic

**Chard** ~ pepper / vinegar

**Corn** ~ pepper / Its flavor too enticing for further additions

**Cucumber** ~ dill / basil / lemon juice

**Eggplant** ~ garlic / onion / pepper / parsley / oregano / mint

**Jerusalem Artichokes** ~ lemon / Tabasco sauce / parsley

**Mushrooms** ~ lemon / horseradish / onion / garlic / pepper

**Okra** ~ pepper / onion / Tabasco / thyme / tarragon / parsley

**Onions** ~ Thyme in a cream sauce. Or bake like a potato, skin and all. No seasoning. Perfection as is.

**Peas** ~ mint

**Potatoes** ~ parsley / dill / lemon / onion / chives / pepper / fennel / caraway

**Rice** ~ curry / saffron / oregano / parsley / pimiento / allspice / rosemary / thyme

**Spinach** ~ nutmeg / vinegar / scallions / marjoram

**Squash (Winter)** ~ pepper (lots) / brown sugar / orange juice and zest / marjoram

**Squash (Summer)** ~ sage / green pepper / onion / basil / pepper / parsley / thyme

**Sweet Potatoes (and Yams)** ~ orange zest / nutmeg / brown sugar / pineapple / cardamom

**Tomatoes** ~ basil / oregano / tarragon / onion

**Turnips** ~ ginger / touch of sugar

**Zucchini** ~ garlic / chives / oregano / parsley / pepper / dill seeds / tomato for acid zip.

# Artichokes (Plan one for each person.)

① Wash artichokes carefully.
② Pull off and discard the tough leaves around base.
③ Cut off most of base stalk, enough so it will stand up nicely on a plate.
④ You may cut off all pointed ends of leaves with scissors if you want to be fancy. I don't bother.
⑤ Lay the artichoke on its side and slice about ¾ inch off the top of the center cone of leaves.

When each artichoke is prepared, as directed above, have a large kettle of boiling water also prepared to receive them. To each quart of water add 1½ teaspoons salt. Be generous with the water. Drop the artichokes therein, cover, and simmer 40 to 45 minutes. Remove artichokes and drain, upside down, in a colander. Cooked artichokes turn a drab olive green color. Don't let that worry you. They may be served hot or cold. Artichokes are usually served as a separate course. I like them with a boiled lobster dinner, for the melted butter is all ready for both the lobster and the artichoke. Its also a delicious combination.

Serve hot with melted butter.
Serve chilled with mayonnaise or hollandaise sauce.

One hopes that guests know how to deal with the choke that covers the heart. If not, be a good teacher.

# Oven-Steamed Asparagus (Serves 4)

### (Easiest of ways to serve this spring delicacy.)

1 pound asparagus, well washed, trimmed, scraped and lined up neatly in buttered, shallow, non-metal baking dish.

dots of butter, arranged on asparagus.

salt and pepper, to your taste

a touch of water, sprinkled over all. (About 1 tablespoon)

Cover snugly with aluminum foil unless you have a tight-fitting lid. Place in preheated 350° oven for about 15 minutes, but fork testing is necessary. It can take up to 25 minutes. The time element depends on thickness of asparagus and the number of people you are serving. I often double this recipe. The asparagus remains wonderfully green and the whole operation uses just one dish. I've also cooked one serving in this manner.

Serve garnished with lemon wedges.

# COOKERY
# CRAFT

As Practiced in 1894 by the Women of the
South Church, St. Johnsbury, Vt.

**STRING BEANS.**

Remove the strings if there are any, break or cut into inch
pieces, cook in salted water from two to three hours, drain.
season with butter, salt, pepper and cream, and serve hot, or
serve cold seasoned with salt as a salad, using a salad dressing.

!

Just so you'll believe me, here's an actual copy from the pages of an 1894 cookbook. It helps to illustrate how mightily our cooking habits have changed in less than 100 years, especially when it comes to vegetables. Imagine taking tender, succulent string beans, fresh from the garden, and boiling them for 3 hours. Heresy.

## String Beans

Here's my favorite way to cook this delicacy: Wash beans before cutting so that good juices are not rinsed away. Then remove the ends. Holding a bunch of beans down with one hand, chop them with a chef's knife into tiny pieces no bigger than a pea. Place the cut beans in a saucepan. Add a bit of water, a dab of butter, a sprinkle of salt. Boil, uncovered, over highest heat about 5 minutes.

Watch carefully. Ideally they should be properly cooked (crunchy-tender) just as water disappears. If any water is left, don't pour it off. Serve as is with a slotted spoon. (Then any leftovers do not become dehydrated.) Or put cooking water in the gravy, or save for soup kettle. As the old cookbook indicates, cold beans can be added to a salad another day. They make a fine addition to a mixed green salad, or give color and crunch to a potato or macaroni salad.

If you have fresh beans, either green or wax, it is gilding the lily to doctor them up with French fried onions, cheese, herbs, sour cream, etc. Save all those embellishments for the canned or frozen variety if so impelled. Serve garden beans with their clean, fresh flavor intact.

~~~~~~~~~~~~~~~

The above type of bean, the common green bean, originated in Central America. The Spanish and Portuguese introduced it to Europe. In time the Europeans completed its round trip by bringing it back to this continent — to North America.

~~~~~~~~~~~~~~~

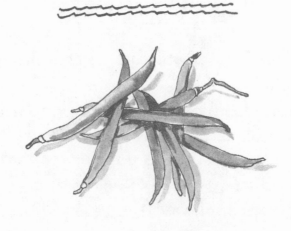

## Miriam's Baked Beets (You'll never boil beets again.)
### 1 pound beets serves about 4.

Wash beets, leaving on the roots and a good inch of top.
Put them into a tightly covered baking dish and bake in
preheated 400° oven until fork tender. Hard to give time
factor, for so much depends on size and age of beets —
probably in the area of an hour, more or less. This makes
the deepest red, sweetest beets ever, all nourishment intact.
Trim and slip off skins when cool enough to handle.
Slice and heat up with a bit of butter and salt and pepper
when ready to serve. (Beets may need a touch of water while baking.)

## Harvard Beets (serves 6)
### The time-honored way to "fancy-up" beets.

¼ cup sugar
1½ teaspoons cornstarch } Mix in saucepan.

¼ cup vinegar
¼ cup water } mixed and stirred into above. Bring to a boil stirring until clear and thickened. Remove from heat at once and to this add

1½ pounds (about) beets, home baked or canned, whole tiny beets or sliced. Mix to coat beets. Put aside until ready to serve.

1 tablespoon butter, added to beets as you heat them through for serving. Correct salt if necessary.

Remember that anything thickened with cornstarch becomes watery if heated too long.

## About Cabbage

Cabbage has been cultivated for 2500 years and was introduced to Britain during the Roman conquest (as were so many herbs). The Romans believed it to be not only fine food but a precaution against the discomforts of high living. Here's what Cato the Elder had to say about it around 200 B.C.:

"The cabbage surpasses all other vegetables. If, at a banquet, you wish to dine a lot and enjoy your dinner, then eat as much cabbage as you wish, seasoned with vinegar, before dinner, and likewise after dinner eat some half dozen leaves. It will make you feel as if you had not eaten, and you can drink as much as you like." (!)

So, with that recommendation here follow two cabbage recipes.

## Just Plain Cabbage
The simplest and probably the best way of preparation.

Cut nice thin shreds of cabbage with a chef's knife, figuring about 1 cup of uncooked cabbage per person. Add a bit of water, salt, pepper, butter. Bring to a boil in open saucepan and boil hard for a very few minutes, chopping and turning with spoon, and hoping you've figured right amount of water so there is none left to pour off when cabbage has become crisp-tender. This is what you might call a stir-steaming technique. Results are excellent. No loss of vitamins or flavor. Serve at once. (For 1 or 2 people, the whole deed is done in about 5 minutes. As quantity increases, for more people, the time element enlarges, of course.)

For convenience, if preparing for company, do all this ahead, undercooking somewhat. Then heat rapidly at last moment.

# Farmer's Cabbage (serves 6)
## A family favorite

about 1 quart shredded cabbage, placed in buttered, shallow baking dish.
2 cups white sauce (page 162), poured over cabbage.
(½ cup grated Parmesan cheese may be added to white sauce but is optional. Delicious either way.)

salt and pepper, to taste

½ cup (about) Ritz cracker crumbs for topping
(Crumbs are more tasty if stirred into some melted butter, but Ritz crackers are fairly rich themselves and will do the job alone if you're butter-shy as I try to be.)

Bake, uncovered, in preheated 350° oven for 20 minutes, no more. Cabbage should still be a bit crunchy.

## Easy Carrots (one large carrot per person)

grate carrots into buttered baking dish. Add:
salt and pepper, to taste
orange marmalade, to taste
butter, a generous dab
water, a splash

Mix, cover. Bake about ½ hour at 350°
Stir once while baking. That's it.

# Creamed Celery* with Water Chestnuts (serves 6)

Butter a baking dish to hold all of the following.

4 cups sliced celery
½ cup water chestnuts, sliced
½ cup sliced mushrooms, fresh or canned
¼ cup slivered almonds

} Put into the buttered baking dish.

4 tablespoons butter, melted in saucepan
4 tablespoons flour, stirred into butter

} Stir this roux until flour well incorporated. Remove from heat.

2 cups milk, stirred into roux until lump-free. Then add:
½ cup grated Parmesan cheese and
½ teaspoon salt      Return to heat and stir constantly
                     until thickened. Pour over vegetables.
                     Mix gently and top with

crushed Ritz crackers in any amount to please you.
        This may all be done ahead of time.
        When ready to serve, bake, uncovered,
        in preheated 350° oven until bubbling
        hot and slightly browned on top —
        about ½ hour.

* Buy pascal (unbleached) celery, if possible. Better tasting, better for you.

## Sautéed Cucumbers

Figuring one average-sized cucumber for each person, peel and cut cucumbers in half lengthwise. With tip of teaspoon remove seeds and cut cukes into chunks. Drop chunks into boiling water for 4 or 5 minutes, no more. Drain and refresh under running cold water. Dry on paper towels. (You may do all this some hours ahead.) When ready to serve, put butter in a frying pan and toss the cucumbers in the butter until heated through and not one bit more. Season with salt — sparingly — freshly ground pepper, and plenty of dill, either fresh or dried.

Cucumbers, of the squash-gourd family, are one of man's oldest foods, and though we are most familiar with them in their raw or pickled states, cooked cucumbers have long ranked high with epicures. I learned the above method of preparation in Julie Danenbaum's cooking class and can recommend it highly. Cucumbers, like many other healthful foods, went through a period of being considered indigestible and appropriate only for "young Persons of an hot and bilious Constitution."

# Mag's Mushroom Casserole (Serves 8 Recipe easily halved.)

1 pound mushrooms, cleaned, trimmed, sliced, sautéed slightly in
¼ pound butter (1 stick)
6 slices white bread, cubed. Place half of the cubes in buttered casserole.

½ cup mayonnaise ⎱
½ cup chopped scallions ⎬ Mix and stir into sautéed mushrooms
½ cup chopped celery ⎭ and pour over above bread cubes. Top with remaining bread cubes.

2 eggs, beaten ⎱ Combine and pour over above. Refrigerate at
1½ cups milk ⎰ least an hour, or overnight if it suits your purposes.

1 can cream of mushroom soup, undiluted, spread over all just
        before baking, uncovered, in preheated 325° oven for
        50 to 60 minutes.

———————

"Deeelicious," says Mag. She's right. This makes a fine
luncheon dish and is good served with peas, dainty
Toasted cheese sandwiches and Tomato Aspic Salad (page 148).
A light fruit dessert would be best.

# Okra    (Serves 4)

<u>1 pound okra</u>, washed, ends cut off, then cut across into about ½ inch slices.

<u>½ cup cornmeal</u> (yellow or white) } Mix this. Then add the
<u>1 medium onion</u>, finely chopped } above prepared okra and
<u>salt and pepper</u>, to taste } toss until thoroughly coated.

<u>corn oil</u> — enough to cover bottom of a skillet. Heat well, but not to smoking, and add above. Cook and stir until slightly browned.

To me, this is the one and only way to cook okra, to which I was introduced somewhat late in life. What a deprivation. In travelling around Arkansas, I never saw a home garden plot that lacked it. And in restaurants where okra was served everyone ordered it. It seems to be a sort of southern addiction. It is one of the few good things that came out of the evil of slavery, first arriving in the U.S. on a slave ship that docked at New Orleans about 1700. The Africans called the okra plant "kinggombo" — a name later shortened to "gumbo." It is low in calories, rich in Vitamins C and A.

Choose small young pods no more than 4 inches long. Cook in aluminum, stainless steel, or enamel ware. Copper, brass, iron or tin causes the okra to turn black, which won't hurt you but is unattractive. Okra is a fine addition to soups or stews, thickening them nicely and creating a "gumbo."

## Little White Onions (1 pound of onions serves 4)

This is a fall rite and an imperative for Thanksgiving and Christmas. They may be served plain in butter or creamed. The latter method is an old New England hangup. Of course it is unnecessary and runs into the turkey gravy on one's plate. But what a delightful conglomeration it is, and it happens only twice a year.

To aid in peeling: Drop the onions in boiling water and boil 1 minute. This loosens the skins. Pour off water and when onions are cool enough to handle, peel. Stab a cross in root end. (This prevents bursting when cooking.) Simmer gently in boiling salted water until tender, about ½ hour. A splash of lemon juice or vinegar added to water helps to keep them white. Onions are now ready to treat in a number of ways.

① When ready to serve, heat up in a bit of butter.

② Make a cream sauce (page 162). Add the onions to it and heat in double boiler.

③ Place creamed onions in buttered baking dish. Top with buttered bread or cracker crumbs. Heat in 350° oven until bubbly.

④ Little cooked onions heated up in real cream and served in separate sauce dishes are an ancient and honorable departure.

## Old-Style Parsnips

Scrape and quarter parsnips, cut in half and
steam until just fork tender, no more.
Transfer to skillet containing hot butter. Sprinkle
with some dark brown sugar (or maple syrup),
salt, pepper. Brown slightly and quickly on
both sides and serve. (Or hold and heat again
at last minute.)

Parsnips are a vegetable one neglects at one's
own sad loss. People either love or hate them. There seems no
middle ground. When the frost begins to leave the ground in
northern New England (just before sugarin') is the time to dig
a mess of parsnips that have stayed in the soil all winter.
This is supposed to ripen and sweeten the vegetable.
I can testify that it does, though I don't hold the old belief that
unless frozen in the ground they are poisonous. Evidently,
the reason for not harvesting parsnips in the fall was that
they did not keep well out of the ground. These days one
can get parsnips almost any time of year in a perfect state
of preservation. But I fear that the thrill of that
early spring "mess" is gone, as is some of the flavor.

Jean's    Parsnips with Apple    (serves 4)

2 tablespoons butter, melted in good-sized skillet.
1 pound parsnips, pared and grated (A food processor is handy).
Place grated parsnips in hot butter along with
2 or 3 tablespoons water and stir-fry about 5 minutes.
Then add:

1 tart red apple, chopped with skin on
1 tablespoon lemon juice
1 tablespoon brown sugar or maple syrup    Stir for another
salt, to taste    3 to 5 minutes
pepper, freshly ground    and serve —
¼ teaspoon ground ginger    even to people who
say they don't like
parsnips.

# Party Peas    (serves 8)

2 ten-ounce packages frozen peas, cooked according to package
        directions. Lean toward undercooking. Drain.
        (The baby petit pois are much the best.)

1 eleven-ounce can mandarin oranges, drained ) Mix with the
1 eight-ounce can water chestnuts, drained, sliced ) slightly cooked peas.

        Heat quickly in a bit of butter when
        ready to serve. Add the slightest touch of

nutmeg

~~~~~~~~~~~~~

      Peas are native to western Asia
and have been important to many parts of the world
as a dried food.    Peas were not eaten in Europe
until the 16th century and fresh green peas were
enjoyed by royalty only.  A mistress of Louis XV of
France recorded her love of that supreme luxury.
How lucky are we of the 20th century!

~~~~~~~~~~~~~

## About Potatoes

While it may be trendy to skip serving potatoes these days, it's hardly merciful. So, while you are peeling potatoes to nourish grateful guests, here's a bit of history to dwell on and some recipes to delight. "Enjoy potatoes and eschew bread" is a good general rule for a dinner party.

―――――――

"Let us eat potatoes and drink water .....rather than submit."
(John Adams in a letter to Abigail in connection with food shortages during the Revolutionary War.)

Potatoes were far from popular in the colonies at the time of the Revolution and Adams' deep concern about the fate of this new country is apparent in recommending such food. And, of course, the water was in place of the taxed tea. White potatoes were "poor man's food" and were a long time becoming acceptable in this country. How different is the feeling today. Almost any man one meets will come up with the cliché, "I'm a meat and potatoes man."

White potatoes are said to have been introduced to New England by Irish settlers who planted some in Andover, Massachusetts, in 1719. It was not until the Civil War that the white potato had become a much-loved and respected staple food, especially in the North. The sweet potato was the staple of the South.

The fact that the white potato belongs to the deadly nightshade family (like the tomato) is perhaps one thing that caused it to be suspect and there has been a persistent superstition that it causes leprosy, of all things! One can find old-timers in Breton villages today who still believe it.*

The French were the last Europeans to accept the potato, but it finally came about as a result of one of those good things that emerge from the evil of war. At the time of the Seven Years' War (called the French and Indian War here), a French pharmacist, Antoine Parmentier, was a prisoner in Germany. Rather than languishing in jail he prospered healthwise and became enthusiastic over the potatoes he was being fed that sustained him so well.

Parmentier's release came just at the time that Louis XVI was worrying about grain riots and food shortages, and he was able to convince the king that an acre of potatoes yielded far more nourishment than an acre of grain. On King Louis' feast day in 1785 a party was given at which potatoes were served for the first time. It was a fashionable gathering and Parmentier had arrived with a bouquet of potato blossoms to present to the king. The story goes that Louis placed some of the flowers in his lapel, handing the rest to Marie Antoinette, who graciously pinned them on her gown. That did it. Potatoes became the "in" thing from then on, chefs vying with each other in outrageous ways of preparing them. Fortunately, also, French cooks had just adopted the English method of grilling beef and it didn't take long to discover what a perfect accompaniment potatoes were. Converts were numerous. Potatoes had arrived.

It was around 1570 that the Spaniards brought the potato (indigenous to Central and South America) from the

* The Horse of Pride by Pierre-Jakez Hélias

new world to the old, a product that could hardly be recognized today. The Incas made a habit of saving the smaller potatoes for seed, which bred them down to minuscule size. Clever European farmers soon developed bigger and better strains. England and Ireland had the potato by about 1610. This proved a great boon to Ireland for over 200 years until the tragedy of the blight and the Great Hunger developed, in what had become almost a one crop economy, in 1845.

~~~~~~~~~~~~~

A few words of advice:

If potato skins are somewhat green, as is often the case, peel deeply, for the green can be toxic. The same is true of potato sprouts, so be thorough in their removal before cooking.

Remember that mealy-type potatoes are best for baking, mashing and such. Waxy potatoes are considered best for potato salad, holding their shape better. If you don't know one type from another here's the test: Make a brine of 1 part salt to 11 parts water. A waxy potato will float in the brine, a mealy potato will sink.

If potatoes mysteriously darken while boiling (known as "stem-end blackening") add cream of tartar to the boiling water (in the proportion of ½ teaspoon cream of tartar to 1 pint water) only after potatoes are half cooked.

This advice comes from Harold McGee's masterpiece, On Food and Cooking.

~~~~~~~~~~~~~

# Bud's Spuds (serves 8)

Especially good with barbecued anything. One potato per person is supposed to be the rule, but my daughter-in-law claims this is never enough. Here's what she did for eight people and there was none left over for breakfast as she had hoped.

<u>12 best Idaho potatoes</u>, skins left on, well scrubbed, put through slicing blade of food processor or sliced by hand neither too thick nor too thin. Arrange in 2 <u>buttered</u>, shallow baking dishes, overlapping somewhat but in <u>one layer only</u>.

<u>2 packages Lipton's Onion Soup Mix</u>, one package to each 6 potatoes, sprinkled over potatoes.

<u>melted butter</u>, in amount your conscience allows, drizzled over all.

<u>dried rosemary</u>, crumbled and sprinkled sparingly over all. (Or use chopped fresh if you have it.)

Bake about <u>45 minutes</u>, or until potatoes are done, in <u>preheated 350° oven</u>. Potatoes should be crisp, not mushy.

    The odors thereby wafted about will have everyone salivating.

    Thank you, Bud Whetstone!

# Potato Favorite

Scrub high grade potatoes and cut up, skins and all, as for fat french fries (about 1 potato per person).

Place in buttered, shallow oven-proof pan and add enough water to come up half way on potatoes.

Sprinkle with salt and pepper and dabs of butter and place pan on burner to bring water just to a boil. Then place in preheated 400° oven on lower shelf. Bake for ½ hour or until water has evaporated.

Remove from oven and turn potatoes over with a spatula. (Undersides should come up golden.) Bake for another ½ hour or until browned becomingly.

I can't recommend this recipe highly enough. Better than french fried potatoes and better for you and no mess with hot fat.    (Corning ware is perfect for this, as it can go from burner to oven to table.)

## Potato Puffs (serves 6)

1 cup cottage cheese ⎫ Beat together in blender or
1 egg ⎬ food processor

3 cups plain mashed potatoes (about) ⎫ Add the above beaten
1 Tablespoon chopped parsley ⎬ cheese and egg to this
½ teaspoon baking powder ⎬ and beat together
salt and pepper, to taste ⎭ thoroughly by hand.

Spoon onto buttered foil, covering a
baking sheet, in 6 mounds. (Or use buttered
stove-to-table shallow dish and serve directly from that.)
Bake in a preheated 350° oven about
20 minutes or until pleasantly browned.

## Potato Pie (serves 6)

3 large baking potatoes, baked at 450° until thoroughly cooked.
Cut in half, scoop out flesh, mash.

1 cup cottage cheese, mashed diligently into potatoes.

¼ cup milk
1 Tablespoon butter
2 eggs, beaten
chopped chives ⎫ If fresh be generous.      Stir into potato mixture.
chopped parsley ⎭ If dried be less so.     (Use salt if you must but I think the
                                            Parmesan gives sufficient saltiness.)
¾ cup Parmesan cheese
¼ cup Parmesan cheese          Mix, then shake around bottom and sides
2 Tablespoons fine, dry bread crumbs   of an 8 or 9 inch pie plate that has
                                        been buttered. Spread potato mixture
                                        in pie plate. This may all be done
                                        hours ahead. When ready to serve,
bake in preheated 350° oven around 40 minutes or until puffy and brown.

Joanne's     <u>Mashed Potato Casserole</u>  (Serves 8)

<u>8 baking-type potatoes</u> , boiled, drained, <u>mashed</u>. <u>No milk</u>

<u>8 ounces softened cream cheese</u> ⎫ Beat this, by hand, thoroughly
<u>1 cup sour cream</u>                  ⎬ into the hot mashed potatoes.
<u>garlic salt</u> , to taste          ⎱ Then plop into buttered baking
<u>onion salt</u>    "   "            ⎰ dish, letting it form nice peaks.
                                        Paint with butter, sprinkle with
                                        paprika.   You may refrigerate
                                        until ready to serve.

Heat in <u>350° oven</u> about <u>20 minutes</u>. Peaks of potatoes should
brown somewhat.

~~~~~~~~~

<u>Plain mashed potatoes</u> (mashed with butter, milk, salt, pepper)
are conveniently served the same way as above and
can be all ready in the morning for the evening meal.
Or they may be heated in a double boiler . Either way
there is no last-minute mess to contend with.

~~~~~~~~~

<u>WARNING</u> : Never try to make mashed potatoes
with an electric beater unless you
are in need of paste. Nothing can take
the place of hand mashing and then
beating with a spoon. The more you
beat the whiter they get.

~~~~~~~~~

Joanne's          Potato Delight  (serves 8 or more)

5 Idaho potatoes, or any high grade mealy potato.
                Boil with skins on, without salt, until tender.
                Refrigerate overnight. (This is vital.)
                Peel the next day. Grate on medium grater
                into a shallow, buttered baking dish.
¼ pound butter (1 stick) melted in saucepan.
                Add to it:

1 pint half and half cream
1 heaping teaspoon salt          Mix and pour over
½ cup grated Parmesan cheese     potatoes, tossing gently.

¼ pound sharp Cheddar cheese, grated and sprinkled over all.

          (This may all be done in the morning.
                Cover, refrigerate.)

When ready for evening meal, bake in preheated 350° oven,
uncovered, about ½ hour.


            This is an Iowa dish. It was served with
steak and a green salad. Memorable. Rich, but worth it.
Taper off with a fruit dessert.


"Mashed potatoes are to give everyone enough."
                                Maurice Sendak

# Sweet Potato and Apple Casserole

Plan 1 potato and 1 apple for 2 people.
You may substitute yams for sweet potatoes.

Peel and cut potatoes in cubes ⎞ Mix well in a bowl.
Peel and cut apples in cubes ⎟ Transfer to buttered
salt, brown sugar, cinnamon ⎟ baking dish.
      added according to taste ⎠
Dot top with butter and add a little water.
Bake, covered, in preheated 350° oven for ½ hour.

Remove cover and bake another ½ hour.

Oh-so-good with ham, pork, veal, poultry.

~~~~~~~~~~~~~~

What is the difference between a sweet potato and a yam?
    What we call yams in the U.S. are really
    a variety of sweet potato. The flesh of the U.S.
    yam is more orange in color, sweeter, more
    moist than the sweet potato. The true yam
    is a native of tropical Asia where it is reputed
    to have been cultivated since about 8000 B.C.!
    Columbus brought the sweet potato (native to Central America)
    from the new world to Europe on his first voyage.
    The sweet potato belongs to the morning glory family.
    The true yam is the tuber of a plant related to lilies.

~~~~~~~~~~~~~~

## Baked Sweet Potatoes or Yams

Don't forget to serve them this easy way. Bake well-scrubbed potatoes at 375° for about an hour or until fork tender. Best to put foil under them, for they are inclined to exude sweet juices which really mess up the oven.

―――――――――

## Twice-Baked Sweet Potatoes or Yams

Cut the baked potatoes in half the long way. Scoop out and mash well with butter, salt, pepper and enough milk for nice consistency. A dash of sherry adds interest but is optional.

For a southern touch: drizzle molasses over each.
For a Vermont accent: drizzle maple syrup.
For kid appeal: put a marshmallow on each.
For simplicity's sake: skip all embellishments.

Twice-baked potatoes, white or sweet, are one of many answers to easy entertaining. They should be all prepared in the morning. When ready to serve in the evening, heat up quickly in a 400° oven.

―――――――――

"The sweet potato provides more calories, minerals and vitamin A (but less protein) than does the white potato."
Food and Cooking by Harold McGee

―――――――――

# Riced Sweet Potatoes (or Yams)

The simplicity of this dish is particularly appealing with meals that include chicken, turkey or pork gravy.

Boil potatoes with skins on in salted water until fork tender. Cool somewhat, then peel. Put manageable-sized pieces, gently, through a ricer (so as not to mash down the "rice") into an attractive, buttered baking dish. You may do this hours ahead of meal. When ready to serve, heat this airy mound in a 375° oven. If it browns slightly, so much the better.

## Sweet Potato Orange Cups

Mash boiled sweets or yams just as you would white potatoes, using orange juice rather than milk. Add salt, pepper, butter, and chopped crystallized ginger to taste. Fill orange halves (which you've saved from breakfast orange juice) and top with a pecan. Arrange in shallow baking dish hours ahead of company. When ready to serve, place in preheated 350° oven for about 15 minutes — or until well heated. A favorite. Decorate with parsley for a handsomely colorful dish.

## Candied Sweet Potatoes

Melt butter and brown sugar over low heat in a frying pan. Add cut-up boiled sweets or yams. Turn to brown on both sides. Add a bit of water if sugar gets too "candied". A New England imperative for holiday meals.

# Ratatouille (serves 6)

(A bountiful harvest of vegetables all in one dish.)

2 tablespoons vegetable oil, heated in large pan.

1 large white onion, sliced ⎫
1 clove garlic, minced   ⎬ Sauté in the oil until tender.

1 medium eggplant, peeled, cubed
3 medium-small zucchini, thickly sliced ⎫ Add to above.
¼ pound fresh mushrooms, cleaned, halved ⎬ Bring to
3 carrots, scraped, sliced                    simmer over
1 small green pepper, cut in strips          low heat, covered,
2 large tomatoes, skinned, cut in chunks     and cook about
2 tablespoons chopped parsley                ½ hour, or until
1 teaspoon salt                              vegetables are
1 teaspoon dried basil (more if fresh)       lightly done.

You may boil quickly, uncovered, to reduce juices at this point.
It is traditional to serve this as is.

    I like, sometimes, to drain the juices, adding
water if necessary to make 1 cup. Mix this with
1 tablespoon corn starch, pour into pan and stir carefully
until thickened and shiny. Adding some soy sauce
is optional but flavorful. Soy sauce is salty, so be careful.
No harm in adding a Chinese touch to a French dish.

# Sauerkraut (serves 4)

Butter a casserole that has a cover.

1 one-pound can sauerkraut, drained and rinsed under running water.

1 cup beef bouillon made with bouillon cube.

1 apple, cut into small pieces (with or without skin, according to preference).

brown sugar, just a little

Combine all in the buttered casserole. Bake, covered, a good half hour in preheated 350° oven.

Best served with pork or ham.

Sauerkraut was brought to Europe from China by the Tartars. There is a persistent mystique concerning sauerkrauts being instrumental in longevity.

## Seven Hints — One for every day of the week.

① A little vinegar, in water in which you boil corn, makes corn more tender.

② Always save potato water for gravy making or bread baking.

③ Try baking corn in the husk in 350° oven for 45 minutes. Picnic-Type fare.

④ Sautéed mushrooms are improved by a squeeze of lemon while cooking.

⑤ One of the best embellishments for cauliflower or asparagus is cracker or bread crumbs heated in butter until slightly browned!

⑥ A colorful and delicious garnish in place of parsley: slices of kiwi resting on slices of tomato.

⑦ When baking potatoes, bake an onion for each person also. Wrap onion, with skin left on, in foil, as it bleeds while baking. It takes the same time to bake as a potato: 1 hour at 450°. Bake tomatoes in last half hour. Cut the top off a tomato for each person. Cut some sharp cheese into strips and poke them into tomatoes which you prop up in contrived foil cups and place in oven for about the last half hour of baking. This can all make most of a dinner, for one or many, that is as effortless as it is delightful.

# Spinach Squares    (Serves 4)

1 ten-ounce package of
    frozen chopped spinach, cooked as directed but without salt

2 eggs, well beaten
1 eight-ounce container sour cream
1 small onion, grated
½ cup grated Parmesan cheese
1 tablespoon flour
1 teaspoon salt
⅛ teaspoon pepper

Mix all this together and then add the cooked spinach above. Stir well. Spread into a 9" x 9" (about) baking dish. Bake uncovered at 350° for 25 to 30 minutes.

This recipe doubles or triples easily, but use a larger baking dish and choose a shallow one. Also, extend baking time somewhat. Cut into squares for serving.

I learned this one in the South and am eternally grateful. It turns even the most obstinate spinach hater into a replica of Popeye the Sailor Man.

# Florentine Tomatoes (serves 6 to 8, depending on Tomato size)

4 tomatoes, cut in half and placed in buttered, shallow baking dish of size to hold them snugly upright. Bake in preheated 325° oven for 10 minutes and then remove from oven.

1 box chopped frozen spinach (10 ounces) (or about 1 pound fresh spinach, cooked from scratch). Frozen spinach cooked as directed on box. Drain cooked spinach thoroughly and season with:

1 tablespoon butter
1 tablespoon chopped onion
salt, pepper, nutmeg, to taste. (Easy on the nutmeg!) } Mound onto partially cooked tomato halves.

Sprinkle generously with:

grated Parmesan cheese ⁓ You may hold at this point as long as is convenient. When ready to serve, bake for at least 10 more minutes at 350°

A delightfully colorful and savory vegetable combination.

Jean Tyson's     Fondue Tomatoes   (serves 6)

6 large tomatoes, tops sliced off, seedy center scooped out,
         turned upside down on paper towels to drain.

2 slices bread, crusts removed

butter
prepared mustard } spread on the bread, then cut into cubes.

4 ounces sharp Cheddar cheese, cubed.

2 eggs, beaten

½ cup milk

1 teaspoon Worcestershire Sauce

2 or 3 drops Tabasco Sauce

onion flakes or grated onion, to taste

salt and pepper, to taste

Mix all this together. Then add the bread and the cheese cubes. Let stand an hour or more. Fill the drained tomatoes with this mixture, first arranging them in proper-sized, buttered, shallow baking dish.
       All this may be done hours ahead.

When serving time approaches, bake in preheated 350° oven, uncovered, for 40 to 50 minutes or until filling is firm and puffy. Serve at once. Decorative and colorful and oh-so-good. Jean served this with individual tenderloins and green beans. A fine luncheon dish. Great to have when the summer supply of tomatoes overwhelms. (A sprig of parsley on each tomato is the final fillip.)

## Surprise Turnip Casserole (serves 10 or 12)

A recipe from Gladys Elviken, who knows more about good cooking and being totally ready for entertaining than anyone I've ever known.

3 pounds Turnips (after peeling), cut up
1 can chicken broth (10 ¾ ounces)
(or 1 ⅓ cups water with one chicken bouillon cube)
} Boil together until turnip is tender. Then mash.

3 tablespoons chopped onion
3 tablespoons chopped parsley
1 cup sweet apple sauce
salt and pepper, to taste
} Stir into the mashed turnips.
Place in buttered casserole and top generously with

Croutons ( page 218)

Bake at 325° until heated through, uncovered.
This is a good make-ahead dish. You may also freeze it successfully.

Man has been sustained by turnips for a good 4000 years, enjoying their tender young greens as well as the purple-white roots. The "yellow turnip" (a misnomer) is correctly called a rutabaga. The rutabaga, a different species than the white turnip, is a recent vegetable on the scene, the first written reference to it being in 1620.

198

# Vegetable Casserole Supreme (serves 6 to 8)
## (Thanks to Polly Cox)

These are "about" measurements. Don't knock yourself out being exact.

1½ cups sliced onion
2 cups celery, coarsely cut
1½ cups carrots, sliced
2 cups green beans, cut small
¾ cup green pepper, coarsely cut
2 cups tomatoes, peeled fresh or canned, with its juice. If fresh tomatoes used, add a bit of water.

4 tablespoons butter, melted
1 tablespoon sugar
3 tablespoons tapioca
1 teaspoon salt

Stir all this together. Place in buttered casserole.
Cover!
Bake 1½ hours at 350°.

A wonderful, shiny (due to tapioca) vegetable feast.
You may add some cauliflower flowerets if you want to.

# Zucchini and Tomatoes Niçoise

A colorful treat at any time of year, but especially in the good old summertime when gardens overproduce.

Slice young zucchini diagonally. Do not peel.
Slice tomatoes vertically. Do not peel.
Lay slices alternately in shallow baking
dish that has been well anointed with vegetable oil.
Brush zucchini and tomatoes carefully with vegetable oil.
Sprinkle over all, salt, freshly ground pepper,
thyme, crumbled bay leaf (a modest touch only),
parsley. (Herbs may be fresh chopped or dried.)

Place in preheated 350° oven for 30 or 40
minutes or until crisp-tender.

～～～～～～～～～

There was a woman in the South who added
oregano to many of her vegetables. Because
this gave them a pizza odor, her kids ate them
without a whimper.

～～～～～～～～～

# Prize Zucchini Casserole (serves 8)

8 young zucchini, diced
1 green pepper, chopped fine
1 good-sized onion, chopped fine
1 cup stale bread crumbs
1 cup grated sharp Cheddar cheese
½ cup oil, olive, corn, or whatever you like
1 teaspoon dried basil (or 3 times that if fresh)
2 eggs, beaten
salt and pepper, to taste

Put all this in a large bowl for easy mixing. (A food processor makes this dish even easier to prepare.)

Stir all together thoroughly. Then transfer to a buttered 9"x13" baking dish. Place, uncovered, in preheated 350° oven for 45 minutes or until nicely tanned on top.

# Scalloped Zucchini (serves 4 to 6)

3 medium zucchini, cut in ½ inch slices and arranged in buttered 9"x13" pan or baking dish.

1 clove garlic, crushed
½ cup mayonnaise

Mix, spread over zucchini slices. Bake, uncovered, in preheated 350° oven for 20 minutes. Remove from oven.

½ cup shredded Cheddar or Swiss Cheese
½ cup bread crumbs
½ teaspoon celery seed

Mix and scatter over partially cooked zucchini. Return to oven and bake another 20 minutes.

(The cheese and mayonnaise seem to supply sufficient saltiness but add salt if you think necessary.)

# VI

# About Bread

The baking of bread not only makes you feel like the most elemental, useful, clever, happy creator, but casts a spell of ecstatic anticipation over your whole household. I know, having indulged in this sorcery for years.

You won't believe this statement but it is a scientific fact perceived intuitively by Hippocrates around 400 B.C. and corroborated by most recent research: "Brown bread is more laxative than white, white more nutritious than brown."*

Sylvester Graham, a minister, sold the country a bill of goods in the late 19th century, lasting into the early 20th century. He claimed that the separation of bran in milling wheat was "putting asunder what God had joined together." He had a point, but we have a way of carrying various fads to an extreme. Graham flour became the rage. John Harvey Kellogg joined in the cry and various whole grain cold cereals were invented. The enthusiasm for same waned somewhat until the mid-1970's when it was revived with a vengeance by a new generation of "health food" enthusiasts and is constantly elaborated upon by the media. Forgotten is the revealing fact that during World War II Dublin was put on whole grain bread for several years and half of the children of that city came down with rickets. So — moderation in all things, even whole wheat. Let's enjoy some good white bread

---

* Page 282 ~ On Food and Cooking by Harold McGee ~ Charles Scribner Sons ~ 1984

without feelings of guilt. We really have been brainwashed.

————————

When flour is called for in any recipes, I mean unbleached. Here in New England we can get King Arthur flour. I'm sure there are other good varieties, but that happens to be a favorite.

For shortening in bread products I use corn oil the most often. Again, you may have a different preference.

I bake bread at a lower temperature than is usually called for. It seems to work better for me. It's so easy to burn the loaves with high temperatures.

Another trick I find useful is to do the last rising of the bread right in the draft-free oven, all ready to bake. Turn on the oven just a second to warm it, then turn off at once. When bread has risen sufficiently, turn on the heat. No need to disturb the fragile, raised dough by moving it from one place to another. A common error is to let dough rise too long, in which case it falls somewhat while baking and doesn't have a nice rounded top. A little experience will tell you when enough rising is enough. In my way of baking it rises a bit more when oven is turned on.

Always turn freshly baked loaves out onto a cooling rack on their sides, and leave them that way.

————————

If you are in the process of selling your house, it pays to have the odor of baking bread wafting about as prospective buyers arrive. I've been told that the house sells every time.

————————

# Batter Bread (1 large or 2 small loaves)

The perfect bread for the beginner. No kneading necessary, just a strong arm. Wonderful, chewy bread or toast.

1¼ cups warm water, poured into large ceramic bowl.
1 package yeast, sprinkled on the water. After a minute or so add:

2 tablespoons sugar
2 tablespoons corn oil
1½ teaspoons salt
2 cups unbleached flour

With a wooden spoon beat this all together with 300 (yes!) vigorous strokes. Best to sit in a chair, hold bowl in lap and look at some mindless T.V. Better than any of Jane Fonda's arm exercises.

⅔ cup of flour, more, stirred in until smooth.

Leaving spoon in bowl, cover and let rise until doubled (About 1 hour). Stir down batter with some meaningful strokes and transfer to buttered bread pan or pans. Let rise until doubled in bulk. Bake at 350° on middle shelf about 35 minutes for small loaves, 45 minutes for large one. Turn off oven and leave loaves therein another 5 or 10 minutes. Turn out onto cooling rack.

## Batter Bread Variations

Add to the yeast-water mixture one of the following:
1. A mixture of 1 teaspoon thyme and oregano and marjoram for Herb Bread.
2. 3 tablespoons instant minced onion for Onion Bread.
3. 3 tablespoons poppy seeds for Poppy Seed Bread.
4. 3 tablespoons sesame seeds for Sesame Bread.
5. 4 ounces sharp Cheddar cheese, grated, for Cheese Bread.

# Easiest Continental Bread (2 long loaves)

Called "continental" because it isn't classic French or Italian or Spanish bread but close to all of them and is ever so basic and satisfactory.

2 cups warm (not hot) water
1 tablespoon (1 package) dry yeast
1 tablespoon sugar
1 tablespoon salt

combine in large bread-making bowl. Stir. Let rest a few minutes. Then gradually add:

flour until it becomes difficult to stir. Turn dough out onto well-floured board and allow to rest before tackling the kneading process. This recipe calls for about 5½ to 6 cups flour all told. (I always use King Arthur unbleached all-purpose flour.)

Good luck with the kneading! You should stick with it for 10 minutes. Place in the original bowl which has been washed and buttered. Butter top of dough. Cover with damp towel. Place in warm location. Let rise until doubled, around 2 hours.

Then punch down and knead out any air. Cut in half. Shape into 2 long loaves. Place on cookie sheet that has been sprinkled with corn meal.

Let rest about 5 minutes. Make a few diagonal slashes in each loaf and paint with cold water.

Place on middle rack of cold oven. Put a roasting pan in bottom of oven and pour some boiling water therein. Turn oven to 400° and bake for 35 to 40 minutes. (No waiting for second rising. This all happens in oven.)

# Three-Egg Bread (2 large or 4 small loaves)

1½ cups milk, scalded — Set aside until cooled to lukewarm.

½ cup warm water, poured into large crockery bowl.

2 packages yeast, sprinkled on the warm water. Let soak a few minutes. Then add the warm milk and the following:

¼ cup (generous) maple syrup or sugar

1 scant tablespoon salt

3 eggs, room temperature, unbeaten

¼ cup corn oil

unbleached flour, enough to be able to beat in with a spoon, but not so much as to tire your arm. (You may add 1 cup graham flour if you want.) Beat all this together diligently with a wooden spoon. Let rest, spoon and all, for about 15 minutes or more.

Now add enough flour to stiffen sufficiently for kneading. Turn out onto bed of flour on board and knead until springy (5 or 10 minutes). Place dough back into crockery bowl which you have washed and buttered. Pat a bit of butter on surface of dough. Place in warm location and cover with dish towel. Let rise until doubled in bulk. Toss back onto kneading surface. Work the air out of it. Cut into 2 or 4 even portions. Pat into 2 big or 4 small well-buttered bread pans. Butter tops. Cover with towel. Allow to rise until doubled. Bake on middle shelf of 350° oven, which you turn on only after bread is in. Bake around 35 minutes for small loaves. More, according to judgment, for large loaves.

# Health Bread (4 hearth loaves)

2 packages dry yeast
½ cup lukewarm water } Soak together in large mixing bowl for about 5 minutes.

1 large potato, peeled and cut up into
2 cups water } Boil until potato is tender. Then mash right in the water. To this watery potato add the following:

6 tablespoons corn oil
½ cup maple syrup
1 tablespoon salt, scant
1 egg
1 cup cold water } Mix well. Add to potato water. Then stir all into yeast in big bowl.

4 cups whole wheat flour
½ cup soy flour
½ cup dried skimmed milk
1 cup sesame seeds, unhulled variety
        or
1 cup nuts, part pecans, part almonds, blended to fine crumbs.
unbleached flour, in quantity needed } Mix well and add to big bowl, stirring long and vigorously. You now have a sponge. Cover, spoon and all, and let rest until puffy. Then add flour until stirring starts to be difficult. Empty onto nice heap of flour. Fence in dough with more flour. Let rest again. Then knead in all the flour necessary for a nice dough. This takes about 10 minutes. (A healthful workout.)

Return well-kneaded dough to big bowl which has been washed and oiled or buttered. Pat top of dough with either fat. Let rise until doubled. Tip out onto lightly floured board. Knead out yeast gases. Cut into 4 equal parts. Pat into round loaves and plop them onto oiled or buttered cookie sheet with sides. Slightly oil or butter the loaves. Slash tops of each one three times with a sharp knife. Let rise until doubled. Put in cold oven. Bake at 350° for around 30 or 40 minutes. You'll find these hearth loaves to be winners. Cool bread on racks.

## Sesame Bread (4 small loaves or 2 large)

1 cup lukewarm water
2 packages yeast
} Place in large mixing bowl. Allow to stand at least 5 minutes. Then stir to dissolve.

1½ cups warm water
2 tablespoons vegetable oil
4 tablespoons maple syrup
(or honey or molasses or brown sugar)
1 tablespoon salt (scant)
} Mix and add to above.

1 cup non-fat dry milk powder
1 cup sesame seeds
½ cup wheat germ
½ cup unprocessed bran
2 cups unbleached flour
} Mix together in another bowl and then stir vigorously into above combination. You now have a sponge rather than a dough. Cover with a dish cloth, spoon and all, and forget it for at least ½ hour.

more unbleached flour (as needed later.)

When sponge has bubbled a bit, add flour until stirring becomes slightly difficult. Then tip the dough out onto a nice bed of flour and knead for about 10 minutes. Place kneaded bread in warm, buttered bowl (the big one you have just used and washed up). Pat dough lovingly with buttered hands. Let rise until doubled in bulk. Turn onto kneading board, knock out the yeasty gases. Divide into loaves and press down into buttered bread pans. (Or shape into round hearth loaves and place on cookie sheet.) Allow to rise in warm location, but don't let rise too much. (Over-risen bread deflates when baked.) Put bread in cold oven. Turn on to 350°. Bake about ½ hour for small loaves, more for large ones. Tip out onto cooling racks almost at once. Excellent bread — and you'll never taste better or more nourishing breakfast toast.

# Feather Rolls (12 large, 24 small)

An old Fannie Farmer favorite that can't be excelled.
No kneading, no shaping, and oh-so-tender.

<u>1 cup warm (not hot) milk</u>, poured into bowl.
<u>1 package yeast</u>, sprinkled on milk, stirred in and
           allowed to rest for 5 minutes.
           Then add:

<u>¼ cup barely melted butter</u>
   (one half of a ¼ pound stick)
2 tablespoons sugar
½ teaspoon salt         Beat this together
1 egg, unbeaten       with an egg beater.
                         Then add:

<u>2 cups unbleached flour</u> ↝ Beat this in, a little at a
                       time, until beating gets
                       difficult. Then stir in the last
                       of flour, by hand, with a
                       wooden spoon.

Cover the bowl, spoon and all. Let rise in warm place
(around 1 hour). Stir down and fill buttered muffin
tins a little more than half full. (I like the small size.)
Cover, let rise for less than 1 hour. Put in 400° oven
(yes, a hot one this time) for about 15 minutes. Watch.
         Always reheat rolls when ready to
serve. Delectable.

## Kitty Grant's Hot Cross Buns

I never had a hot cross bun "turn me on" until Kitty served these. Easter season has been brighter ever since.

2 packages yeast, soaked in ½ cup warm water while doing what follows.

½ cup vegetable oil
¼ cup milk         } Combine in large mixing bowl.
¾ teaspoon salt    } To this mixture add:
⅓ cup sugar

1 cup unbleached flour   } that have been well mixed together.
1 teaspoon cinnamon      }

3 eggs, beaten and added to big mixing bowl along with the yeast mixture. Stir mightily.

3 cups unbleached flour } combined, and stirred and stirred into
⅔ cup currants          } above. The more you beat this dough the better. (If too stiff, add a touch of warm water.)

Cover bowl with damp cloth and allow to rise in warm location until doubled in bulk — about 1½ hours. Punch down and scrape out onto floured board. Allow to rest 10 minutes. Roll or pat to 1 inch thickness. Cut with biscuit cutter into nice rounds. Place on buttered baking sheet 1½ inches apart. Let rise until doubled (about 1 hour). Cut cross in each bun with sharp blade. 1 egg white, slightly beaten with which you brush each bun lightly. Save what is left of egg white and mix with ¾ cup confectioners' sugar, sifted. Hold. Bake buns at 375° for 15 minutes. Cool. Then frost the crosses.

# Apple Muffins (one dozen)

Oh-so-good on a frosty morning.

1 egg
½ cup sugar, white or brown
4 tablespoons corn oil
1 cup milk
} Toss all in a bowl and combine with egg beater.

2 cups flour (half whole wheat if you want)
3 teaspoons baking powder
½ teaspoon salt
} Mix together well in bowl of size for whole recipe. Using sifter is probably best. The aim is to have the baking powder and salt totally dispersed. Pour liquid mixture above into this. Stir sparingly and add at once!

1 cup chopped, peeled apple ~ Stir apple in lightly and spoon batter into well-buttered muffin tins, making them about ⅔ full. (Leave apple skin on if you wish.)

2 tablespoons sugar
1 teaspoon cinnamon
} Have ready mixed and spoon a little heap onto each muffin. Rake it into surface of muffin with a fork.

Bake in preheated 400° oven about 20 minutes.
You may bake this batter in an 8" square buttered pan if too hurried to do the muffin routine. Cut in squares. Paper cups for muffins may save work but are a no-no. A good muffin must be crisp and crunchy with that wonderful flavor a buttered muffin tin imparts.

~~~~~~~~~

See next page for a true muffin horror story.

I know an old man in Danville, Vermont, whose mother always made muffins for breakfast. This is what he told me: "Pa regularly started a good fire in the wood stove as he headed for the barn, early to milk, so Ma had no excuse not to bake muffins that we all loved. One morning she came into the kitchen, as usual, and there was a hot fire burning accompanied by the most frightful smell, and smoke pouring out of the oven. With sinking heart she opened the oven door which she'd left ajar the night before to heat the kitchen. Sure enough, her pet cat had found a warm place to sleep, but hardly planning on eternal rest. Ma had a hard time to forgive Pa for not bein' more noticin' — and it was a week or so before she had the heart to make any more muffins."

This will not exactly whet your appetite for breakfast muffins but the telling may help me exorcise a true tale which has haunted me for a long while. Poor "Pa" just never thought to look in the oven before slamming the door shut. Poor cat!

# Banana Bread    (1 loaf)

## (Less sugar, no fat)

3 ripe bananas, well mashed ⎫ Mix in bowl.
2 eggs, well beaten _____⎭

2 cups flour ⎫
½ cup sugar ⎪ Sift together into above.
½ teaspoon salt ⎬
1 teaspoon soda ⎭

½ cup nuts (walnuts or pecans), chopped and added to batter.
Pour into buttered bread pan and bake in preheated 350° oven for 1 hour.
Remove from pan and cool on rack.

~~~~~~~~~~~~~~~~~

There were evidently some bananas in Charleston, South Carolina, by 1850, for Fredrika Bremer, a Swedish novelist visiting there, wrote, "Bananas, Negroes, and Negro songs are the greatest refreshments of the mind ..... which I found in the United States."

Others found them refreshments of the body also, especially after the Philadelphia Centennial Exposition of 1876, where bananas, a great novelty, were sold for 10¢ apiece. Because bananas spoil so rapidly, they could not be shipped any distance until refrigerated ships and railroad cars came along. Today, with bananas available every day of the year, everywhere, we are inclined to forget how brand new is the accessibility of this once-considered-exotic, tropical fruit.

~~~~~~~~~~~~~~~~~

Agnes Barry's  Cranberry Bread (1 large loaf, but preferably 2 smaller ones)

1 cup cranberries, ground up slightly in food processor or blender. Put ground, fresh berries aside. Stir into batter at the very last.

1 cup sugar
2 cups flour
½ teaspoon salt
½ teaspoon baking soda
1½ teaspoons baking powder

Sift all this into bowl large enough for whole recipe.

½ cup (or more) chopped pecans or walnuts, stirred into above flour mixture.

1 egg, beaten, and to it add what follows:
2 tablespoons corn oil
grated rind of orange, to equal about 1 tablespoon
This is optional but adds deliciousness.
¾ cup orange juice (stretch with water if necessary.)
½ teaspoon vanilla

Mix well. Then stir into dry ingredients above! Bake in buttered bread pan or pans in preheated 350° oven for 1 hour. Bread slices more easily when a day old. Who cares? It's elegant right away.

In sailing ship days Englishmen took limes or lemons to sea to ward off scurvy. New Englanders took cranberries, which are a fine source of vitamin C and potassium. Half of the annual cranberry crop in the U.S. comes from Massachusetts.

When Benjamin Franklin went to France at the beginning of the American Revolution, he wrote home for "barrels of such curiosities (to the French) as cranberries and butternuts for the Queen (Marie Antoinette)."
(From Louis and Antoinette by Vincent Cronin)

# Cranberry Muffins (makes 12 or more average-sized muffins)

⅔ cup whole wheat flour
⅔ cup unbleached all-purpose flour
1½ teaspoons baking powder
¼ teaspoon salt
1 cup sugar

} Place a sifter in a bowl large enough for whole recipe. Sift. Hold.

1 egg, well beaten
grated rind of 1 orange
juice of same orange
¼ cup vegetable oil

} Mix together and stir into flour mixture only when what follows is prepared.

1 cup cranberries (fresh or frozen), chopped
  (You may substitute 1 eight-ounce can of whole cranberry sauce, in which case reduce sugar to ½ cup.)

½ cup nuts (pecans or walnuts), chopped

} I do this in food processor. Blender can also be used but processor is more satisfactory. Stir into batter. (Should batter seem too thick add water.)

Bake in buttered muffin tins in preheated 400° oven about 25 minutes, filling each section ⅔ full.

Be sure to put some cranberries in your freezer when crop is at its height in the fall. Freeze it in package in which it comes from the store, securing it in another plastic bag for better protection than just one covering. Wash, in their frozen state, just before using, never before freezing or they stick together.

## Johnny Cake   (Serves 6)
### (The easy, modern way.)

1 cup yellow corn meal
½ cup unbleached flour      } Measure into small
2 teaspoons baking powder  } bowl and hold.
½ teaspoon salt

½ cup milk
½ cup maple syrup
1 egg
2 tablespoons corn oil

) Measure directly into blender
  and blend well.
  Then add the corn meal mixture.
  Blend only until mixed, not a
  second more. Pour into buttered
  8" square baking pan or corn stick
pan or muffin tins.

Bake in preheated 450° oven for 20 minutes for the
square cake, less, according to your judgment for other
alternatives.

You may substitute brown or white sugar for
the maple syrup. And use less sweetening if you are so
inclined. It won't taste quite as good, but good enough.

It was a happy day when I discovered that
this favorite old recipe could be created in seconds
in a blender.

# Newfangled Corn Bread (Serves 6 or 8)

1 cup unbleached all-purpose flour
1 cup yellow corn meal
4 teaspoons baking powder
½ teaspoon salt
2 tablespoons sugar

} Mix well in bowl large enough for whole recipe.

6 ounces sharp Cheddar cheese, grated medium-fine and stirred into above.

2 eggs, large, beaten
⅓ cup milk
¼ cup vegetable oil
one 4-ounce can green chilies, drained, chopped
one 8½ ounce can cream-style corn

} Mix this all together in another bowl, then empty into above! Stir until just moist, no more.

Spread into 9" square buttered pan. Bake in preheated 400° oven about 35 minutes.

Place on cooling rack. Cut in squares and serve while still warm. Or cool and reheat at your convenience. Serve with soup or salad and you have a whole meal.

Come summer, I plan to use a cup of corn cut fresh from the ear, some chopped green pepper in place of the chilies, and a bit of maple syrup for sweetening. The more I think of it the more possibilities come to mind! Why didn't I think of fancying up corn bread before this? (chopped onion, for instance!) This recipe seems an invitation to innovation.

Louise's    Quick Beer Biscuits

1 cup Bisquick (for each 2 people), placed in bowl.
1 tablespoon of sweetening or less (maple syrup, honey,
              brown or white sugar — you choose).
beer — enough of your favorite variety to make a stiff
       dough. Beat enthusiastically with a spoon.
       Plop onto buttered baking sheet in any size
       spoonfuls you want. Bake in preheated
       400° oven for 10 to 15 minutes!
This makes the tenderest biscuits in just a jiffy.
(I often use ¾ cup Bisquick to ¼ cup wheat germ
when on a health kick.)

Croutons — (Indispensable for soups
              and salads.)
       The best kind are made at home. Don't fry them,
bake them. A good way to use up stale bread.
       Cut bread, with or without crusts, into small cubes.
Transfer to a fairly deep baking dish (so they can be stirred
without spilling over). Dot with butter for plain croutons.
Sprinkle with herbs for herbed croutons, in any combination
that appeals to you. Dot with butter also. (If you've made
Sidney's Herb Seasoning, page 286, you're in clover.)
Put in 250° oven and stir well when butter has melted.
Stir, maybe once more, as croutons bake slowly. It takes
about 1 hour. They should be palest tan, not dark, or they
taste bitter. Keep in air tight container.

# 90-90's  Cottage Cheese Pancakes (makes about 12 pancakes)

3 eggs  put into a bowl and beaten well.

1 cup cottage cheese, drained of any liquid ⎫ Stir all this into
2 tablespoons corn oil (or melted butter) ⎬ eggs. Drop batter
by not-too-large
¼ cup flour (yes, that's all) ⎫ spoonfuls onto heated
griddle, about 350°.
¼ teaspoon salt

- - - - - - - - - - -

Turn carefully, browning delicately on both sides. (Cooking takes longer than traditional pancakes.)

This makes a lovely breakfast treat served with maple syrup and bacon or sausage. They are angel-wing tender and low in calories. (If you live alone, use one egg and the rest of ingredients in proportion.)

~~~~~~~~~~~~

This recipe was given me many years ago by a delightful man named Metcalf Melcher (sp?). He was more or less courting my widowed aunt who was in her 80's and the suitor crowding 90. They drove to my Vermont farm one weekend from Boston to visit me. Aware of their ages, it was with relief that I saw their safe approach. My aunt greeted me in her usual lively fashion despite the walker that held her up. Around the car from the driver's seat came Mr. Melcher, leaning

on a cane. I shook his hand warmly and said,
"How happy I am to meet you, Mr. Melcher." He
replied, "Oh, don't call me Mr. Melcher — call
me Go-go." (!) His vitality and enthusiasm for
everything soon made it apparent why his
grandchildren had given him such a nickname.

    The next day, at breakfast, he initiated
me into the mystery of these pancakes, which will
ever remind me of that gallant old boy. I've
since found the recipe in Fannie Farmer's Cookbook,
so that makes it a classic.

~~~~~~~~~~

**Barbara Clark's** <u>**Buttermilk Pancakes**</u> (Serves 8 — a recipe
easily cut in half!)

4 cups flour  
4 teaspoons baking powder  
2 teaspoons baking soda    } Sift this together into a
2 teaspoons salt        bowl, preferably the night
½ cup sugar           before serving. (Then you're
all set for a firehouse start
in the A.M.)

4 eggs, beaten, to which add } Mix, then pour onto above
1 quart buttermilk       flour mixture. Stir gently and
½ cup vegetable oil      let it rest a bit before spooning
onto hot griddle.

Barbara says this is the most popular breakfast for skiers
at her Quechee, Vermont, hideaway. She serves the pancakes
with <u>butter</u> and <u>syrup</u> (room temperature, not heated!) and <u>sausage</u>.

~~~~~~~~~~

# Virile Pancakes   (serves 4)

½ cup warm water, placed in mixing bowl.
2 packages dried yeast, sprinkled over the water and allowed to
rest while you heat:

2 cups milk, heated to lukewarm only along with ⎫ Pour this
1 tablespoon maple syrup (or sugar)                ⎬ mixture into
½ teaspoon salt                                     ⎭ yeast.

2 eggs                                        ⎫ Add to above and
2 teaspoons corn oil (or any vegetable oil)    ⎬ beat with egg beater
2 cups flour (half whole wheat if you prefer)  ⎭ until all is thoroughly
                                                 blended.

Place this batter in warm location, cover with towel and forget it
for an hour. It should be all bubbly and lovely by then. Spoon
onto griddle gently — and there you are.

These pancakes are a different texture than
the packaged variety but I like them better and so did our forebears.
I have read that many old-timers were upset by the invention of
baking powder and the consequent neglect of yeast, believing
that this would diminish their manhood. Therefore the name
I have given them.

Serve with butter and maple syrup, of course,
and with sausage or bacon. And please don't heat the syrup!
That is heresy. It turns the syrup to water and the pancakes
to mush. If plates are hot and syrup at room temperature
the situation is perfect.

If you mix up this recipe the minute you
roll out of bed in the morning you have just the right amount
of time to bathe, dress, make your bed and the pancakes
are ready to cook. Exactly one hour is not imperative.

It can be more or less. If it begins to foam over the bowl and you're not ready to cook them, stir down and let rise again.

If you have any batter leftover, stir down, cover, refrigerate, and, when you get good and ready, add more flour and make drop biscuits. Stir in enough flour to make a good doughy consistency and put spoonfuls of the dough onto buttered cookie sheet. Let rise and bake in 350° oven. Batter will keep for days in refrigerator.

The above pancake recipe is easily halved for 2 people or doubled for a larger group or redoubled endlessly for a gang. No half-used boxes of pancake mix sitting around for six months. We are conned into buying a lot of unnecessary stuff.

# Cake ~ Cookies

# Three Purpose Banana* Batter

① Banana Cake ～ ② Banana Loaf Bread ～ ③ Banana Muffins

¼ pound stick of butter (or ½ cup vegetable oil), creamed with
1 cup sugar, and beaten together well in large beater bowl.
2 eggs, added one at a time and beaten in well.
2 medium bananas, ripe, mashed, and beaten into above.

2 cups flour
1 teaspoon baking soda      } Sift this together into above and
½ teaspoon salt              mix well.
½ teaspoon cinnamon         } After incorporating flour mixture,
                             stir in:

½ teaspoon lemon extract (or 1 tablespoon lemon juice)
½ teaspoon vanilla
½ teaspoon grated lemon rind
½ cup chopped pecans or walnuts

① For the cake: Bake in 8" or 9" square buttered pan in preheated
        350° oven for about 40 minutes. When baked, slice
        2 bananas over top of cake and sprinkle bananas
        with a covering of 2 tablespoons melted butter mixed
        with ½ cup brown sugar and ¼ cup flaked coconut.
        Slide under broiler for about 2 minutes or until bubbly. Fantastic.
② For Banana Loaf: Pour batter into buttered bread pan. Bake at 350°
        about 55 minutes. Cool on rack for a spell before
        turning out.
③ For Muffins: Butter 24 small muffin pans and spoon batter
        therein. Bake at 350° around 15 or 20 minutes.

* You may use frozen bananas. See page 4.

# 14-Carat Carrot Cake (serves 10 to 20 or more depending on size of pieces.)

2 cups finely grated carrots
one 8½ ounce can crushed pineapple, drained
one 3¼ ounce can flaked coconut
½ cup chopped nuts, pecans, almonds, or macadamia(!)

} prepare, mix, hold

2 cups flour
2 teaspoons baking powder
1½ teaspoons baking soda
1 teaspoon salt
2 teaspoons cinnamon

} Sift together into mixing bowl.

4 eggs, well beaten, then stir in:
2 cups sugar
1½ cups oil (I use corn.)
2 teaspoons vanilla

} Stir this vigorously into above flour mixture. Then do likewise with the waiting carrot mixture. Pour into well-buttered and floured pan or pans of your choice. Bake in preheated 325° oven for 45 minutes. Cool before frosting.

If you want a layer cake to bring to the table in all its glory for a birthday or such, use 3 round eight or nine-inch layer cake pans. Otherwise use one 9"x 13" pan if you want a lot of cake squares to serve as dessert for a group. This is the easier way and can produce 20 or 24 pieces. On the unlikely chance there's leftover cake, it keeps beautifully refrigerated or frozen. This puts any other carrot cake in the shade.

## Cream Cheese Frosting

½ cup butter (one ¼ pound stick), softened
one eight ounce package cream cheese, softened
2 teaspoons vanilla
1 one-pound package confectioners' sugar, sifted

} mix thoroughly until smooth and spreadable, Then frost the cooled carrot cake.

# Viennese Chocolate Layer Cake  (Serves 10 or 12)

The dark, moist, sinful variety that should appear in every home on rare, special occasions.

4 one-ounce squares of unsweetened chocolate  } Melt together slowly in saucepan of size to hold whole recipe. Cool somewhat,
4 tablespoons butter (½ of a quarter-pound stick) }

2 cups flour
2 cups sugar
1 teaspoon salt, scant  } Sift into chocolate. Mix well.

1½ cups milk
1 teaspoon vanilla
1 egg, unbeaten  } Add to above, beating with spoon, with might and main, until smooth as silk.

¼ cup milk
1 teaspoon soda  } Mix milk and soda and then, quickly and thoroughly stir it into the batter.

Pour batter into two 9-inch layer cake pans lined on the bottoms, with waxed paper. Bake on middle shelf of preheated 350° oven for exactly 40 minutes. Cool on racks before removing from pans. Remove and cool on racks, totally, before frosting.

## Chocolate Icing

2 one-ounce squares unsweetened chocolate, melted slowly, cooled a little.
1½ cups confectioners' sugar
½ cup (¼ pound) soft butter (not melted)
1 teaspoon vanilla
1 teaspoon lemon juice
salt, a shake
1 well-beaten egg

Add this, in order given, to chocolate. Beat until smooth. (If too runny to spread, add more sugar.) Fold in nuts at the last. Spread frosting between layers and on top and sides. This will make you a hero in your own home.

1 cup nuts (of your choice) that have been slightly roasted and chopped fine. (I prefer pecans or almonds.)

# Moist Orange Cake (Serves 12)

(Rich, sweet, irresistible, but why bother to make a cake that isn't?)

3/4 cup soft butter (1½ sticks), creamed thoroughly with
1 cup sugar ⟶ Then add all of the following which you've prepared
ahead:

2 eggs, well beaten
1 cup sour cream
grated rind of 1 orange, large, thick skinned. Grate onto a
piece of waxed paper. (Wash orange well first.)

1 teaspoon soda
2 cups flour } sifted together
1 teaspoon vanilla
1 cup dark, seedless raisins

½ cup chopped pecans that have been roasted, before chopping,
in 325° oven (in pie plate) for about 15 minutes,
for maximum goodness.

Pour well-mixed batter into buttered sponge cake pan
(tube pan). Bake in preheated 350° oven exactly 1 hour.
Cool cake in pan on rack for 10 minutes before inverting.
Leave cake in inverted pan until completely cool (several hours).
Then remove from pan and place right side up on serving
dish.

juice of ½ orange with
½ cup sugar dissolved therein. } Spoon this sweet juice carefully over every bit of top of cake, allowing to drizzle down sides somewhat.

Cover. It keeps for days and freezes well.

# Quick Norwegian Almond Crisps (makes about 30 cookies)

½ stick butter (¼ cup), softened

½ cup sugar

1 egg, unbeaten

3 tablespoons flour, level

1 teaspoon vanilla

Salt, a sprinkle

1 cup slivered almonds
(the kind with skins still on)

Toss all this into a small bowl in order given, mixing each addition thoroughly. Place small dabs of this batter (no more than a teaspoon) onto well-buttered and floured cookie sheet, each dab 2 inches apart.

Bake in preheated 400° oven for 5 minutes on center shelf of oven. After 5 minutes check the cookies constantly. They may bear another minute or so of cooking. Remove from oven and, where cookies have run together, mark with a sharp knife. Wait about 3 minutes before removing cookies with spatula to cooling rack. This seemingly small recipe must be done in two editions. After first half is done, I wipe the cookie sheet with a paper towel and quickly butter and flour it for the second go-around. The cookie batter is made in minutes but its care after that takes some time and skill.

Keep cookies tightly boxed in a cool place. Or freeze them.

# Susan Houle's Baklava (around 40 hauntingly delicious pieces)

Have ready: ① cookie sheet with sides (11" x 17" is good size) ~ ② pastry brush ~
③ sharp serrated knife ~ ④ several sheets of newspaper

Syrup: Make ahead and chill, preferably overnight.

> 3 cups sugar
> 2 cups water
> 2 cinnamon sticks

Bring to boil. Then add:

½ cup honey   and boil gently 2 to 3 minutes. Remove from heat and add:

½ teaspoon lemon juice ~ Syrup is now ready to be chilled.

Pastry:
> 1 pound fillo leaves ("Apollo" recommended)
> 1 pound butter, melted and kept warm
> 1 pound walnuts
> ½ teaspoon cinnamon

finely ground together (Food processor is great for this.)

Preheat oven to 325° to 350°

Set-up as pictured →
(Cover fillo with Saran Wrap if it starts to dry out as you work with it.)

ground walnuts
melted butter

Step 1: Brush cookie sheet with melted butter.

Step 2: Put 2 leaves of fillo on cookie sheet and brush with butter. Repeat this step 2 more times — producing 6 leaves of buttered fillo.

Step 3: Now add 2 more leaves of fillo brushed with butter and sprinkle with ground nuts. Continue this sequence of 2 buttered fillo plus walnuts until walnuts are used up — saving 6 leaves of fillo for topping exactly as in step 2. But do not butter top layer of fillo until you have cut it.

Step 4: Cut as pictured below, right. Diamonds seem to be most satisfactory but make any shape you want.

Step 5: After cutting, brush top with butter carefully.

Step 6: Bake at 325° to 350° until top puffs and begins to turn golden. (About ½ hour at the most.)

Step 7: Now reduce heat to 250° and bake a total of 2 hours. (This includes above timing.)

Step 8: Remove from oven and pour chilled syrup over hot baklava. Allow to rest several hours.

This will keep at room temperature a week or more. Better to freeze it if kept longer. When speaking of "food for the gods," baklava should top the list.

# Date Cookies
## (Healthful, fat-free, chewy fruit bars)

7 Graham crackers, crushed
1 cup pecans or walnuts (measured before chopping)
1 cup unblanched almonds          "        "        "

This may be done in food processor, adding crackers first and turning them into crumbs, then adding nuts to chop lightly. Empty into mixing bowl and add in order given:

½ cup sugar
1 teaspoon baking powder
pinch of salt
2 eggs, well beaten
1 teaspoon vanilla
1 package dates (about 10 ounces net),
     pitted and cut into small pieces
     with scissors dipped in water.

Mix all together well and press into 9" x 13" pan. Bake on middle shelf of preheated 325° oven for ½ hour. Cut into squares or bars while still warm and transfer them with spatula to cooling rack. Store in tight container or freeze for future use. Great for kids coming in from school, along with a glass of milk.

I find dates too sticky for food processor chopping so enjoy doing them the slow, old-fashioned way to improve my time while watching T.V.

# Hello Dollies (about 36 squares)

(From The Centennial Cookbook of Trinity Episcopal Church, Collinsville, Connecticut. Trust a church to come up with a cookie as sinfully good as this.)

¼ pound stick butter, melted in 9"x 13" shallow pan. When butter is melted, tilt the pan in all directions to butter the sides.

1½ cups graham cracker crumbs, sprinkled evenly over the melted butter.

1 cup chopped nuts (walnuts or pecans or almonds)

1 cup chocolate bits or morsels or buds

1⅓ cups flaked coconut

1 can sweetened condensed milk (about 14 ounces)

} Sprinkle all this as evenly as possible over the butter-cracker layer, one layer at a time, in exact order given.

Bake in preheated 350° oven for 25 minutes.

Allow to cool somewhat on rack before marking off into squares.

Let cool even more before removing.

I use my sharp dough scraper pictured on page 298 to cut these cookies because I can press directly down rather than drawing a knife across, which is inclined to make cookies a bit ragged on the edges. Do it carefully with a sharp knife and all will be well. I wrap squares separately in waxed paper and refrigerate for short term holding, or freeze for long term.

232

## Go-to-bed Cookies (makes around 30 or 40 dainty, crunchy delights.)
### (Thank you, Julia Fifield.)

Preheat oven at 350° while making the following in minutes:

2 egg whites, beaten stiff while adding gradually:
⅔ cup granulated sugar ~ When thoroughly beaten,
                    fold in by hand:
1 six-ounce package semi-sweet, small, real chocolate bits
                    or morsels or buds or chips and

¾ cup Rice Krispies

     Butter a large cookie sheet. From a teaspoon, push off little dabs of above mixture onto cookie sheet. If you want one-bite size, make 40 or more dabs; two-bite size, make about 30 dabs. Put them as close together as you want for they keep their shape nicely and do not spread. Put into preheated 350° oven and allow to bake exactly one minute. Then turn off the oven and go to bed. No peeking! Reward cometh in the morning when you lift off the cookies and store in airtight container. The simplicity of this operation is exceeded only by the excellence of the result. Nice tea party fare!

     My sister likes to serve these with Coffee Jelly (page 253) for dessert. A mocha treat.

# Health Cookies (Makes a great quantity and you'll be glad of it.)

½ cup vegetable oil
1 cup dark brown sugar
½ cup molasses
2 eggs (no need to beat)
½ cup water
1 Tablespoon vanilla
1 teaspoon lemon extract

Toss into very large bowl and mix with might and main.

1 heaping cup whole wheat flour
1 cup wheat germ
¼ cup soy flour
1 teaspoon salt
½ teaspoon baking soda
1 heaping teaspoon cinnamon
1 teaspoon clove
1 teaspoon allspice
1 teaspoon nutmeg
3 cups uncooked oatmeal
1 cup sesame seeds
½ cup sunflower seeds
1 cup coconut
1 cup chopped nuts (I like pecans and/or almonds best.)
1 fifteen-ounce box seedless raisins

Put all this into another large bowl. Mix thoroughly with your hands. Then stir into above. It's a rather dense mixture.
Add some water if you must. Drop by well-heaped teaspoon onto buttered cookie sheets. Then go over each cookie with wet fingers — shaping and firming. (This is as important as it is time consuming.) Bake in 350° oven for 10 to 15 minutes. Watch! Bake only to delicate tan.

Please see next page for more Health Cookie talk.

## <u>Health Cookies</u> — continued

If two cookie sheets are in the oven at the same time, be sure to exchange their locations half-way through the baking for uniform results. When baked remove from oven and allow to cool slightly. Then scoop off onto cooling racks. Keep enough for immediate use in refrigerator in plastic bag. Freeze the rest in convenient-sized amounts ready for the moment of need. These cookies make a meal with a glass of milk. Great to have on hand for those who would skip breakfast. If your school child has some of these in the lunch box, nutritional needs are met without the kids suspecting it because they taste so good.

Don't let the formidable array of ingredients put you off. If you lack one or two things called for, don't worry, they will still be good. They are basically an oatmeal cookie loaded with nourishment, delicious in flavor, and an aid to digestion second to none. Take them on auto trips. Take them as a hostess gift that will never be damned by faint praise.

# Hermits

(I cut them to make about 32 hermits. Make large or small according to your needs.)

2 cups flour, all-purpose, unbleached
½ teaspoon salt
⅔ teaspoon baking soda
⅔ teaspoon cream of tartar
1 heaping teaspoon cinnamon
1 heaping teaspoon ginger
½ teaspoon nutmeg
½ teaspoon cloves
½ teaspoon allspice

} Sift this all together in bowl large enough for whole recipe.

⅓ cup citron or candied orange or grapefruit peel, chopped
1 cup raisins (or half raisins, half currants)
½ cup nuts of your choice, chopped

} Mix and then stir into flour mixture above.

½ cup sugar
½ cup corn oil
½ cup molasses
2 eggs

Stir together, then beat well with egg beater and pour into all of the above. Mix thoroughly. Pour into well-buttered jelly roll pan (16" x 11") (or 2 smaller pans). Spread batter evenly. If batter too stiff, add a touch of water. Bake in preheated 350° oven for about 15 minutes or until lightly done. Cut into generous squares while warm.

Fragrant, spicy hermits are said to have originated on Cape Cod in the days of clipper ships. Packed in tole canisters, they must have been highly valued and have made the roughest voyage endurable. They are a far cry from the weevily hardtack we read about. Hermits are claimed to be the forerunners of brownies. Both are recommended for a happy voyage through life. And a cinch to make.
They freeze well.

# TOTAL Brownies (16 squares)

2 eggs
1 cup sugar } beaten together thoroughly.

½ cup flour, stirred into above.

½ cup butter (¼ pound)
2 ounces unsweetened chocolate
(usually 2 squares, but they sometimes
differ in size and weight.) } melted together in double boiler and then stirred into above when slightly cooled. (You don't want to cook the eggs!)

1 tablespoon vanilla
salt — only a sprinkle
1 cup (or 6 ounces) semi-sweet chocolate bits
½ cup chopped nuts, walnuts or pecans or almonds } stirred into above and turned into 9" square pan that has been well buttered.

(An optional but elegant touch, if almonds are used, is to sprinkle another ½ cup chopped almonds over the batter in pan, pressing them in a bit.)

Bake in preheated 350° oven for about 25 minutes. Don't overcook. Allow to cool somewhat and cut into squares.

Chocolate lovers will love you dearly if you serve these. For storage, each square should be wrapped separately, especially if you freeze them, which they take to nicely!

Dorothy Keys'    Lemon Ice Box Cookies

½ pound butter (2 sticks) ⎫
½ cup brown sugar (dark) ⎬ Cream together thoroughly.
½ cup white sugar ⎭ Then beat in all the
following ingredients:

1 egg
1 tablespoon grated lemon rind
3 tablespoons lemon juice
2 cups unbleached flour, sifted with
¼ teaspoon baking soda
1 cup finely chopped pecans

When all is well mixed, shape into
two elongated, cylindrical rolls
and wrap them in waxed paper.
Refrigerate overnight or longer.
Slice into satisfactory cookie
thickness and place on greased
cookie sheets. Bake in preheated
350° oven for about 10 minutes
or until very slightly tanned.
Cool somewhat, on rack, before
removing. These cookies freeze
beautifully.

The term "Ice Box" reveals the age of this recipe.
It came from Texas.

## Magic Macaroons (makes about 2 dozen)

2 cups shredded coconut

(The dry, unsweetened kind available at health food stores is best. But any kind will do.)

½ cup sweetened condensed milk

Mix and drop by teaspoon onto well-buttered cookie sheet. Use fork to pat down and press into neat rounds. Bake in preheated 350° oven on the top shelf for about 10 minutes.

They should be a delicate tan, no more. When somewhat cooled remove cookies with spatula onto cooling racks. Store tightly covered or freeze.

Delicious, and what a cinch to make! Your three-year-old could do this. I double the recipe and then don't need to wonder what to do with the leftover condensed milk.

Whenever I use condensed milk I think of the true story my friend, Rosamond Loeb, told me. She went to a dinner party where a very delicious pie was served for dessert. The hostess kindly shared the recipe. The main ingredient was condensed milk. Rosamond likewise served it with great success and decided she should send the recipe to the manufacturer of the milk, thinking she had latched onto something really original. She sent it to the president of the company. (Which company I have forgotten.) In short order she received a whole case of condensed milk, along with a gracious letter from the president, thanking her for her thoughtfulness, but letting her know that the recipe in question had appeared on their label some ten years before.

Which leads me to the suggestion that it's always a good idea to read labels. I've picked up many a fine recipe that way.

# Dorothy Keys' Chocolate Macaroons
### (about 36 cookies)

2 squares bitter chocolate, melted in top of double boiler.

1 fourteen-ounce can condensed milk

2 teaspoons vanilla

1 seven-ounce can or package shredded sweet coconut

1 cup chopped pecans

Salt — just a delicate shake

Stir into melted chocolate in order given.

Drop above mixture by heaping teaspoons onto well-buttered cookie sheet. Bake in preheated 325° oven for exactly 20 minutes. Set cookie sheet on rack to cool slightly. Then remove cookies from pan and cool them completely on rack. Store in airtight container. (They are crisp when first cooled but soften properly in container.) Cookies keep well, freeze well. Excellent! Great with orange sherbet or any orange dessert.

(Here's a suggestion in case you have the time and/or strength to strive for perfection: Toast coconut and pecans together in shallow pan before mixing cookies — in a 325° oven, stirring often, as coconut browns fast. You want a delicate tan. The cookies are wonderful without this added effort, so don't let this hint worry you.)

Jean Rowland's    Swedish Oatmeal Cookies (makes about 36)

¼ pound butter, heated slowly in saucepan large enough for whole recipe.

½ cup brown sugar
½ cup white sugar
1 cup flour
½ cup quick-cooking raw oatmeal
1 egg, unbeaten
1 teaspoon vanilla

Add all this in order given, to melted butter. Stir vigorously. Drop by teaspoonful onto foil covered cookie sheet. No need to butter foil. Bake in preheated 350° oven for 12 to 13 minutes at the most, on middle shelf. Watch! Don't overcook. Cool and then peel off from foil, which is accomplished easily. Bake in two editions so as to have consistent results from using middle shelf.

You can make these in the time it takes to read the directions on a box of "store-bought" cookie mix. And there's no cookie sheet to wash.

"The modern child needs less
head shrinking and more cookie baking."

# Peanut Crisps

¼ cup butter (½ of a ¼ pound stick), melted in very large kettle.

1 ten-ounce package marshmallows (about 40 large marshmallows
or 4 cups miniature marshmallows)

Place marshmallows in the melted butter and
heat slowly, stirring often, until marshmallows
are completely melted.

6 cups Rice Krispies

1 eight-ounce jar peanuts (Planters)
(Dry roasted and unsalted preferred,
unless you crave salt. You may also
substitute Planters Sunflower Nuts
if so inclined.)

Stir this into the
melted marshmallows
while still on low
burner. Remove
from heat the minute
it is properly mixed.

Turn into buttered 13"×9" pan and press into place
with buttered fingers. When cool, cut into squares
or oblongs.

The whole thing is liable to be devoured
at once. But for any leftovers or for gift giving it
is best to wrap the crisps separately in waxed paper
or plastic wrap and refrigerate.

This recipe is one of those bonuses gained
from reading the side of a Kellogg's Rice Krispies box.
Only I add more peanuts. Easy to become an addict.

# Pineapple Puffs (about 25 cookies)

1 eight-ounce can crushed pineapple, drained ever so
      slightly in strainer. Do not press out juice.
      Set aside.

1 five-ounce package Stella D'oro Anginetti cookies
      ( Look for Italian flag on both ends of
      plastic package.) Cut cookies in half,
      crosswise, with serrated knife. Put aside.

1 three-ounce package cream cheese, softened   Mix together
                                   thoroughly. You
1 cup Cool Whip (Non-Dairy Topping)      may do this in
                                     beater bowl.
                               ( I find it easier to do
                               with potato masher.)

To the blended cheese and Cool Whip add the
pineapple. Stir well. Then with teaspoon
well heaped with this mixture, fill the base
of the cookies, which have an indentation that is
just right to receive the filling. The filling
is adequate in amount for all the puffs.
Now press tops of all the cookies firmly
onto filled puffs.

Arrange completed cookies in covered container and
keep refrigerated until ready to serve. They will
disappear like dew before the sun. Seldom is anything
so good so little work.

# Muriel Manning's Potato Chip Cookies (makes about 75 cookies)

1 pound soft butter
1 cup sugar
1 overflowing tablespoon vanilla
} Cream together thoroughly.

3 cups flour
2 cups coarsely crushed potato chips
1½ cups chopped pecans
} Add to above in order given.

Roll into balls the size of a walnut. Place on buttered cookie sheet. Flatten with hands or fork, allowing room for them to spread in baking. Bake in preheated 350° oven for 12 minutes. Cool slightly, loosen with spatula, but keep on cookie sheet until frosted:

## Frosting

3 tablespoons soft butter
juice of ½ orange
2 teaspoons lemon extract
3 cups confectioners' 10-X sugar sifted
} Mix all together until properly spreadable. Add a touch of water if necessary. ½ teaspoon frosting to each cookie should see you through.

These are lethally good cookies, loaded with things we're warned against. But doctors and psychiatrists agree that everyone needs a "circus day" now and then. So bake these cookies for that uninhibited day in your life! They freeze well.

## Praline Cookies, Texas style (makes about 52)

graham crackers carefully broken apart along marking lines and arranged tight together to fill an unbuttered cookie sheet. I get 52 sections on mine.

1 stick (¼ pound) butter ———————
1 cup dark brown sugar, packed down } Put in saucepan and heat and stir until butter is melted and sugar is lump-free.
2 tablespoons milk ———————
(No need to boil, just close to it.)

2 cups coarsely chopped pecans, stirred into above. Then spoon this nut-sugar mixture carefully over the crackers, guiding the crackers with your finger so they don't separate. Sit down to do this, for it takes a bit of time and patience to cover crackers thoroughly. (Any exposed edges will get too brown.)

Place on middle shelf of oven under preheated broiler and broil until mixture bubbles — no more! Watch. 2 or 3 minutes does the job. Remove from oven. Allow to cool before lifting from cookie sheet with small spatula.

Sarah Creedle served these cookies with a fresh fruit dessert at a special luncheon in Fredericksburg, Texas. Everyone was avid for the recipe. Sarah obliged.

# Snowballs*

(Makes about 4 dozen inch-in-diameter spherical cookies.)

½ cup butter (¼ pound or 1 stick), melted in large, heavy saucepan.
Remove from fire and stir in:

1 cup sugar
1 cup chopped dates
1 egg, broken directly into saucepan and stirred vigorously.
Now put back over low heat and simmer for
10 minutes, stirring almost constantly. Cool somewhat,
but while still warm add:

1 teaspoon pure vanilla
½ cup chopped nuts (walnuts or pecans)
3 cups Rice Crispies
Mix well, and with buttered hands pinch off
portions sufficient to form into one-inch balls.
Drop them onto
coconut that is finely shredded and has been spread onto
waxed paper. Roll in the coconut until well coated.

Store in tight container. They keep well, freeze well, are
a cinch to make, are ever so delicious with a chewy-crunchy
goodness. And you have but one pan and one spoon to wash in the
clean-up operation. (Well, a French knife for chopping.)

* A Christmas tradition in Agnes Barry's family. And no wonder.
Wait until you taste them!

## Sunflower Seed Cookies (Makes about 60 cookies.)

1 cup sunflower seeds, coarsely chopped (Blender or processor can help.)
1½ sticks (¾ cup) butter, softened
1½ cups dark brown sugar
1¼ cups flour
¼ teaspoon baking powder
¼ teaspoon salt
1 egg, beaten

Mix well and then add the sunflower seeds. Form into ½ inch balls with hands and place on buttered cookie sheets, pressing down with fork. I use 3 sheets, for the cookies spread alarmingly, so should be placed far apart. They make the most delicate lace-like cookies. (Of course you can keep using the same cookie sheet over and over.) If cookies do run together, don't worry. Cut into squares. They lift off easily. Bake in preheated 300° oven about 15 minutes or until edges are browned. Serve with a plain fruit dessert.

~~~~~~~~~~

We once had a neighbor, much beloved, who was grossly overweight, sedentary to a degree and a non-coper in all departments of life. She and her husband took their main meal each day at the local hotel, bringing home sandwiches to tide them over for another twenty-four hours. Strangely, she was a health-food devotee and augmented their hotel fare with all sorts of nuts, seeds and capsules between meals. One day she remarked, "I don't dare eat too many sunflower seeds for they give me such a sense of well-being that I'm afraid I might overdo." We waited in vain for some evidence of overdoing. Sunflower seeds will forever remind me of her classic remark.

Here's hoping these cookies will impart a "sense of well-being" to you.

~~~~~~~~~~

# VIII

## Dessert

# Dessert Ideas

Here are some quick, light and lovely desserts that never fail to please:

watermelon, cut into bite-sized pieces )  Mix and transfer to your
fresh sage leaves, chopped fine )  prettiest glass bowl.
maple syrup, just a touch )  Chill thoroughly. I never
served anything that elicited
more enthusiasm than this.

### Sister Mag's Dessert

fresh blueberries )
Sour cream )  Mix, chill and serve to appreciative guests.
maple syrup )

No time to fuss over dessert? Put some vanilla ice cream
in punch cup or tumbler or tall glass. Pour over it some
ginger ale and serve with spoon of appropriate length.
Nothing new about this combination but it is ever so refreshing
and, for some reason or other, always surprises.

Chopped crystalized ginger, added to any fruit, fresh or stewed or
canned or mixed in various combinations, lifts them out of
the ordinary. So does a topping of meringue. Saving a
couple of egg whites you don't know what to do with?

2 egg whites, at room temperature, beaten until stiff.
2 tablespoons sugar, added slowly toward last
of beating. (This is less sugar than usually recommended
but I think its enough.)

Put meringue on buttered foil in blobs. Bake at 325°
about 10 or 15 minutes, until a pretty tan. Remove from
foil with pancake lifter and embellish any dessert that
calls for improvement.

Shredded coconut added to meringue, before
baking, is a tempting touch, especially with pineapple.

~~~~~~~~~~~~

Float meringue on Soft Custard (page 254) and you've
produced an old-time favorite: Floating Island.
You may also serve the beaten, sweetened egg whites
on custard without baking, but it must be served at once,
before it sags.

~~~~~~~~~~~~

Nothing is more work or more delicious than fresh orange
sections mixed with peeled and seeded grapes. A dessert
for a special love.

~~~~~~~~~~~~

To peel oranges and grapefruit more easily, pour
boiling water over them and let soak for 5 minutes.
It also helps in removing segments from membrane.

~~~~~~~~~~~~

# Apple Pandowdy (Serves 4)

A dessert recipe that came to us with the earliest English settlers. Mentioned appreciatively by Nathaniel Hawthorne. It endures for its goodness and is especially popular with those who avoid pastry.

Cut crusts from enough slices of thin white bread (I use Pepperidge Extra Thin) to cover the bottom and top of the baking dish of your choice. Butter the baking dish and sprinkle sugar lightly over the butter. Butter the bread and place it butter side down in the bottom of baking dish, fitting it in nicely so dish is completely covered.

3 tablespoons molasses
⅓ cup brown sugar
2 tablespoons lemon juice
2 tablespoons dark rum          } Mix together well in bowl
1 Tablespoon (yes!) vanilla        large enough to receive
½ teaspoon cinnamon                the apples.
¼ teaspoon nutmeg

apples, cut 3 large or 4 medium-sized into quarters.
Peel, core carefully, slice very thin into above mixture.
Stir until well coated and transfer onto bread in baking dish.

Now arrange buttered bread, butter side up, on top of apple mixture. Sprinkle sparingly with sugar. Place in preheated 375° oven for about ½ hour or until crust is golden brown. Serve warm, passing a pitcher of cream. (If indifferent to tradition, serve with vanilla ice cream.)

# Applesauce Crisp (saves the day!)

It was one of those days of unexpected company and no time to shop. What to have for dessert for hungry young people? I had plenty of apple sauce, some in the refrigerator, some frozen, but that didn't seem enough of a treat. It was the kind I call stewed apples and not put through a strainer. Here's how:

Quarter, peel, and remove all core thoroughly of as many apples as you want. (Figure about 1 apple per person.) Put the quarters in a saucepan with a little water, maple syrup, and lemon juice. Simmer, covered, until apples are tender. Add cinnamon to your liking. This makes a textured apple sauce that many prefer to the strained variety.

Having enough of this apple sauce on hand, I put it in a buttered baking dish, ready to heat somewhat at serving time. In another baking dish I melted some butter and into the butter tossed some bread cubes until well coated and baked them in a 300° oven until crisp and lightly browned. (To make the bread cubes, pile up as many slices of bread as you desire and with a chef's knife cut one way then another to achieve the size of croutons you want. This takes seconds only. )

At serving time the croutons were spread in a generous coating on the warm apple sauce. This was topped with mounds of vanilla ice cream. This slightly tart-crunch-sweet was a sensation and I've been serving it regularly ever since the emergency induced it. (This treatment should be equally good with stewed peaches or blueberries.)

# Rena's Apple Crisp  (serves 6)

(One elegant dessert generously shared with me by Elaine Parker.)

6 large apples, peeled, cored and sliced into buttered baking dish.

1 cup flour  
1 cup sugar  
1 teaspoon baking powder  
½ teaspoon salt

Mix thoroughly in bowl.

Break over the top of this mixture:

1 egg, and, with your hands, mix all together carefully. Then, with fingers, crumble over the apples.

2 tablespoons melted butter  
2 tablespoons milk

Combine and spoon over flour mixture.

cinnamon, sprinkled evenly, in judicious amount, overall. Bake uncovered in preheated 350° oven for 45 minutes or more. Serve warm with

## Rena's Lemon Sauce

½ cup sugar  
1 tablespoon cornstarch  
salt, a shake

Mix together in saucepan. Stir in slowly

1 cup cold water — Cook over low heat, stirring until clear. Remove from heat and stir in:

1 tablespoon butter  
grated rind 2 lemons  
6 tablespoons lemon juice

Serve at room temperature.

# Blueberry Flummery (serves 6 to 8)

This recipe is so old as to be new. It came with the first settlers from the British Isles, where it was called "Summer Pudding" and was made with strawberries and raspberries also. I like blueberries best, perhaps because that is the variety on which I was brought up.

4 cups (1 quart) blueberries, washed )  Mix in saucepan.
1 cup sugar                          )  Bring slowly to simmer.
2 tablespoons lemon juice            )  Simmer about 5 minutes.
¼ teaspoon cinnamon                  )

8 slices bread, crusts removed, buttered    (Be sure to butter baking dish.)
Line the bottom of baking dish with bread. Spoon on the hot fruit, then layer bread and fruit alternately until all is used, ending with fruit as top layer. Bake for 20 minutes in preheated 350° oven. Chill. Serve with pitcher of cream.

## Coffee Jelly (serves 6)

Another ancient and honorable dessert invented, no doubt, in the spirit of "waste not, want not," solving the problem of what to do with leftover coffee. It was my father's favorite.

1 envelope unflavored gelatin, soaked in
½ cup cold water for about 5 minutes. Over this pour
2 cups very strong coffee, boiling hot. Stir until gelatin totally dissolved.
Pour into an oiled mold, the prettier the better.
Chill, unmold, serve with cream and sugar.
(There are those who would appreciate the use of decaffeinated coffee.)

# Blender Soft Custard (Serves 6)

2 cups milk
3 eggs
6 tablespoons sugar
⅛ teaspoon salt
1 tablespoon flour

While water is coming to a boil in the bottom of a double boiler, toss these ingredients into blender. Blend thoroughly. Transfer to top of double boiler. Stir and stir over boiling water until the custard coats spoon and begins to thicken. Remove from heat at once and stir in

1 tablespoon vanilla (yes!)

Cover and refrigerate immediately. (It thickens more as it cools.) Lean toward undercooking custard. The minute it is overcooked it curdles.

You now have the perfect sauce to embellish many desserts:

① Pour it over all sorts of fresh, stewed or jellied fruits and puddings.

② Plop some meringue* on a dish of Soft Custard and you have Floating Island. In this case you'll want egg whites. So, use 4 egg yolks in the custard instead of 3 whole eggs and you'll be all set. There are often times when whites are needed and a custard made with just yolks is equally good, some think better.

③ Pour custard over jelly roll moistened with sherry and you have an English Trifle.

④ Add more sugar, vanilla and plenty of cream and you have the makings of the finest vanilla ice cream.

⑤ Add some cooked rice and raisins and you have a Rice Pudding.

Soft Custard is less rich than whipped cream and a substitute that always delights. Or perhaps I should say that whipped cream is an unfortunate substitute for Soft Custard, which seems to be almost forgotten these days.

★ See about meringues — (pages 248, 249 and 125, 126)

# Carefree Custard

(Serves 6 to 8, depending on size of custard cups.)

1 fourteen-ounce can sweetened condensed milk

2 cans warm water (This a great "two birds with
(from faucet)    one stone" deal — measuring
and cleaning out can at same time.)

3 eggs

1 teaspoon vanilla

Toss all this into blender in order given. Blend well. Pour into custard cups or 1 quart baking dish.

nutmeg, grated generously onto custard.

Place cups or baking dish in shallow pan and add hot water to pan to depth of at least 1 inch. Place in 325° oven for about 45 minutes. Better to undercook than overcook custard. Remember that custard continues to firm up somewhat as it cools. I try to remove it from oven when it's still a bit "wavy" when you nudge the pan.

This produces the smoothest custard. Serve with crisp cookies as accompaniment.

Fresh grated nutmeg is so much better than the stuff that is already ground and has been sitting on your spice shelf for too long.

# Easter Nests (makes about 15)

A happy tradition in the family of Rose Mans.

1 twelve-ounce package real chocolate bits,
melted in double boiler.

9 regular shredded wheat biscuits,
broken up fine enough that you think
a bird might like to build a nest of it.
Stir into the melted chocolate.

Now begins the fun and mess. With buttered fingers and the
aid of a spoon, form this mixture, on waxed paper, into
little individual nests while still warm and pliable.
Fill each nest immediately with
jelly bean eggs in all colors obtainable. Press the
eggs down a bit while nests are
still warm. They stay put better.

These little nests, full of bright colored eggs, are not only
decorative — they're pleasantly edible. And small fry
love to help with their creation. One nest at each
place setting makes a festive Easter dinner table.

# Never Fail Pie Crust

I have tried almost every pastry recipe that exists, hoping to come up with something even easier and better than the one in Bentley Farm Cookbook. No way. So here it is again:

2 cups flour
1 teaspoon salt
½ cup cold corn oil
¼ cup cold milk

Stir together lightly. Form into a ball with your hands. Place between sheets of waxed paper and roll out to desired size. Never chill before rolling. Once pastry is arranged in pie plate, then chill it.

This recipe is more than enough for a one-crust pie. Use the leftovers for little tarts. I don't make 2-crust pies for I've never found the bottom crust to be crisp enough to suit me.

The best pies start in a prebaked shell. Or pastry topping a deep dish pie is always crisp. Always butter a pie dish before pressing in the pastry for both bottom and top crust pies. Easier to serve and to wash the dish later on.

For baking pie shell alone, cook in preheated 475° oven for about 10 minutes. For deep dish pies, such as apple or blueberry, bake at 450° for 10 minutes, then turn oven down to 350° and and bake 50 to 60 minutes more.

---

Speaking of corn oil, always keep it or any vegetable oil in refrigerator.

A touch of vegetable oil, added to butter in which you may be frying, keeps butter from smoking.

And speaking of butter, we often avoid buying sweet butter because it spoils so fast in refrigerator. Keep an emergency supply in freezer, taking out a little at a time as needed.

---

Dorothy Keys' Heavenly Pie (Truly heavenly)
Make 24 hours ahead

1 baked pie shell (see previous page)

2 egg whites
½ teaspoon vinegar
½ teaspoon cinnamon   } Beat until stiff but not dry.
¼ teaspoon salt

½ cup sugar, added gradually to above. Beat until very stiff.
       Spread in pie crust. Bake at 325° for 15 to 18 minutes.
       Cool to room temperature.

Melt:
1 six-ounce package chocolate chips
(real chocolate, semi-sweet morsels or bits)        Carefully spread
2 egg yolks )                                       3 tablespoons of this
½ cup water } mixed together well                   mixture on the cooled
            and stirred thoroughly                  meringue above. Chill
            into melted chocolate.                  remaining mixture until thick.
            Stir until smooth.

1 cup heavy cream, whipped with:
¼ cup sugar                         Fold into above chilled
¼ teaspoon cinnamon                 chocolate mixture and spread
                                    over top of pie. Refrigerate
                                    at least 24 hours.

Try it. You won't like it — you'll love it!

# Peachy Pie  (serves 6)

1 nine-inch baked pie shell  (page 257)

1 eight-ounce package cream cheese, softened  ⎫ Mix well.
2 tablespoons sugar                                              ⎬ Spread in baked
2 tablespoons milk                                               ⎪ and cooled pie shell.
¼ teaspoon almond extract (no more!)      ⎭ Chill in refrigerator.

2 ten-ounce packages frozen peaches, well thawed, well drained,
reserving juice.
Arrange peaches on
chilled pie.

⅔ cup peach juice          ⎫
1 tablespoon cornstarch  ⎬ Mix and stir over heat until
¼ cup sugar                     ⎪ clear and thick.
1 tablespoon lemon juice ⎭

1 tablespoon butter, stirred into hot peach mixture, then
cooled as quickly as possible and poured
over peaches. Chill the pie until
serving time.

This is a peachy dessert and not rich.

# Pear or Peach Melba (serves 4)

A colorful, quick and easy dessert that always makes a hit.

Use canned or home preserved fruit.
Put ½ a pear or peach in sauce dish.
In the fruit cavity put a mound of vanilla
ice cream or some softened cream cheese.
Either treatment is a treat. Then pour
over some cold Melba sauce:

1 ten-ounce box frozen raspberries, thawed
and forced through strainer or twisted in
cheese cloth. In the proportion of 1 cup juice
to 1 tablespoon cornstarch, mix juice and
cornstarch together. Bring to a boil, stirring
until clear and thickened. This all happens
in seconds. Add some sugar if you want.
Chill and it is ready for serving.
(The amount of juice you get varies —
probably a scant cup, so use a scant tablespoon of
cornstarch.)

# Classic Indian Pudding (Serves 4 to 6)

Considered the oldest New England dessert and one of the best. It was cooked on Saturdays in a slow oven along with the beans.

3 cups cold milk (whole or skimmed)  } Stir together in saucepan until
4 tablespoons yellow corn meal } lump free. Bring to boil, stirring often. Remove from heat and add:

1 tablespoon butter
¼ cup sugar
½ cup dark, unsulphured molasses

1 egg, beaten with
¼ teaspoon salt
¾ teaspoon ginger
¾ teaspoon cinnamon

When all this has been stirred into above, pour it into a buttered baking dish. Bake in 300° oven for ½ hour — uncovered. Then remove from oven and pour over it gently:

1 cup cold milk (A strange rite that makes a more tender pudding.)
Then return to oven for 2 hours at 300° or 3 hours at 250°.

Let it sit for ½ hour after removing from the oven. Then serve it in its state of warm perfection with a pitcher of plain cream. Or you may wish to go modern and have a dip of vanilla ice cream melting over each serving. Joy of Cooking calls this "barbarous". I call it beautiful. Then there are non-conformers who like whipped cream or hard sauce. Any leftover pudding may be heated up another day.

Indian Pudding is basically a milk pudding, so it "wheys" or separates somewhat, as it is supposed to. This makes for tenderness and brings on thoughts of Little Miss Muffitt as one savors it. Heretics have been known to add more corn meal to prevent wheying. They deserve the tough, dry results.

One of the "in" things to do when visiting Boston is to go to Durgin-Park's restaurant and have Indian Pudding for dessert. Why not have the same fun at home?

# Hungarian Plum Cake (Serves 6) or 8
### (thanks to Betty Parks)

½ cup (¼ pound) soft butter  
½ cup sugar  
} Cream together, then add the following:

2 eggs, well beaten

½ teaspoon almond extract

1 cup all-purpose flour  
¼ teaspoon salt  
1 teaspoon baking powder  
} Mix together and stir thoroughly into above. Then pour into buttered glass or ceramic pie plate.

10 pitted plums*, arranged on the batter skin side down. Then sprinkle the plums with:

½ cup sugar  
1 teaspoon cinnamon  
} mixed together

Bake in preheated 400° oven for ½ hour.  
Better place something under pie plate to catch any possible drips.  
Serve warm with whipped cream or vanilla ice cream.

When plums abound in the late summer, be sure to try this recipe. You'll be rewarded.

* I use the purple "prune plums" but believe any variety of plum would be fine. And it occurs to me that a generous topping of blueberries or blackberries might prove excellent substitutes. Use your biggest, deepest pie plate. Or a shallow baking dish of any shape would do!

# Prune Whip   (serves 6 to 8)

<u>1 package</u> (1 tablespoon) <u>unflavored gelatin</u>, soaked in
<u>¼ cup water</u>  for at least <u>5 minutes</u>

<u>juice from stewed prunes</u> } combined to equal 1½ cups.
<u>juice of 1 lemon</u> _ _ _ _ _ } If not adequate quantity
add water to make it so. Bring this to
boil, pour over gelatin, stir until thoroughly dissolved.

<u>2 cups pitted stewed prunes</u> } Put in blender with all of
<u>1 teaspoon lemon extract or some grated rind</u> } above.  Blend well.
of lemon

<u>4 egg whites</u>, beaten until stiff. Then fold into prune mixture along with:
<u>¾ cup sugar</u> , about — you be the judge of sweetness.
<u>touch of salt</u>

Plop into your prettiest glass bowl. Cover. Refrigerate.
Serve with <u>Custard Sauce</u> (page 254) which makes
use of those 4 egg yolks.

This is a dainty, healthful dessert that can be made a day or so
in advance of company. This old New England standby
is always enthusiastically received. Our Puritan forebears
evidently were not aware that " The Elizabethans . . . . .
thought so well of prunes [as aphrodisiacs] that they served
them as free lunches in their brothels."

# Rhubarb Pudding (Serves 4 to 6)

Rhubarb, long considered a necessary spring tonic, appears in this guise as a necessary delight. Use pink (strawberry) rhubarb if possible. This is an old-time recipe prized by those who eschew pastry.

Cut rhubarb into small pieces until you have 1 quart. Place layer of rhubarb in buttered baking dish. Sprinkle generously with sugar and coarse bread crumbs and dots of butter. Repeat these layers until rhubarb is used up, ending with crumbs and butter.

Bake in preheated 375° oven for about 40 minutes or until crumbs are brown and rhubarb tender. Serve warm with plain or whipped cream.

Or even better: go very lightly on the sugar and serve with maple syrup!

# Summer Puddings

### (As English as one can get.)

For the strawberry, raspberry, blueberry season. (The frozen variety will do if you lack the fresh-picked.)

Line a well-rounded bowl completely with bread trimmed of crusts but not buttered. This takes a bit of cutting and fitting and some overlapping is desired, just so no part of bowl is exposed. Prepare enough of the fruit of your choice to fill the bowl, washing and draining it and adding sugar to your taste. Toss berries about until sugar is dissolved and juices drawn somewhat. Then pour into the bread-lined bowl and fit more bread carefully over the top.

       Find a plate of right size to sit on top of pudding. Place a weight thereon (the heavier the better). Refrigerate overnight at the least; longer is better. When ready to serve, turn out onto your best serving dish. It should make a brilliant red or blue mound. Serve with cream, whipped or plain.

I like to make this dessert for Fourth of July with either strawberries or raspberries, on one of my "flowing blue" plates, surrounded by whipped cream — a striking red, white and blue delicacy of such simplicity as to be elegant.

George the Third wouldn't like this — turning a distinctly English dish into a Fourth of July celebration.

# Snow Pudding  (serves 6)

This is the lightest and most refreshing dessert. Don't fail to serve it.
Esteemed by the Victorians.

1 envelope plain gelatin ⎫
¼ cup cold water ⎬ Soak together for about 5 minutes.

1 cup boiling water, poured over soaked gelatin and stirred and
stirred* until dissolved.

1 cup sugar, stirred into above.

grated rind of 1 lemon ⎫ Or use both. The more lemony the better.
          or          ⎬ But if you're feeling too frail to grate
½ teaspoon lemon extract ⎭ the lemon, just the extract will
                           get you by. Add to above.

¼ cup lemon juice ⎫ Stir into above. Refrigerate just until
¼ teaspoon salt ⎬ syrupy, no more.

4 egg whites, room temperature, beaten until stiff.
         Then beat the syrupy gelatin mixture until fluffy and
         fold gently into egg whites. Transfer to best glass bowl.
         Refrigerate until ready to serve along with a pitcher
         of Soft Custard (page 254), which you'll make with
         the four remaining egg yolks.

* The reason I'm forever emphasizing the careful, total dissolving of
gelatin is because I actually know people who can't make anything
jelled come out right, not even Jell-O. Incredible but true. I presume
the difficulty is due to lack of patience and eyesight when it comes
to the dissolving process.

# IX

## Preserves — Sauces — Miscellaneous

## Onion Sauce or Soubise (2 cups)
### (By the blender method)

4 tablespoons butter, melted in pan

3 medium onions, coarsely chopped, cooked in above butter, covered, on low heat until soft. Transfer to blender along with:

3 tablespoons flour
1½ cups milk
salt and pepper, to taste
¼ teaspoon nutmeg

Blend, pour into top of double boiler and heat over boiling water, stirring until thickened. Cool, covered, to prevent skin forming.

Reheat when ready to serve.

Makes an excellent gravy for bird, beast or fish that seems too dry. This turns any cooked vegetable into a special treat. Add chopped hard-boiled eggs and/or cooked ham and serve on toast.

## Mock Hollandaise (A little over 1 cup)

1 cup milk
2 tablespoons flour
salt and pepper, to taste
or
a chicken bouillon cube
(or both)

Whirl in blender. Transfer to double boiler. Stir until thickened and smooth.

Now add:

6 tablespoons butter, stirring until it melts.

2 egg yolks
1 tablespoon lemon juice

Beat together and stir into above. Cook about 1 minute if you plan to serve at once. Otherwise remove from heat immediately and hold all day if need be.

When ready to serve, heat over boiling water until good and hot but no more. Remember, this is in the custard category and overcooking can cause it to curdle.

How about making Go-to-bed Cookies, page 232, with the left over egg whites?

# Chattanooga Horseradish Sauce

one 16-ounce jar pineapple preserve
    or jam
one 16-ounce jar apple jelly          } Mix well in blender.
one 8- to 10-ounce jar horseradish    } Keep refrigerated.
2 or 3 teaspoons dry mustard

This innocent-looking mixture, which resembles apple sauce, has an enormous punch. It will clear your head, make your eyes water. It is deliciously different served with beef or ham.

Don't worry if you can't find the ingredients in the exact weights indicated. Make an approximation thereof. As one uses it in small doses, it lasts a long time. Put some of it in little containers and distribute as gifts if you can bear to part with it.

## Horseradish Relish Mold (Serves 8 or more.)

1 three-ounce package lemon gelatin
¾ teaspoon salt } Place in bowl.

- - - - - - -

1 cup boiling water, poured over gelatin and salt.
Stir until thoroughly dissolved.
Then add:
1 tablespoon vinegar and
pepper, a good dash, freshly ground.
Chill until slightly thickened but not jelled.

1 cup sour cream or yogurt
½ cup prepared horseradish
1 tablespoon, generous, grated fresh onion } Mix and stir into slightly thickened mixture above.

Transfer into one oiled mold or 8 individual.
Refrigerate until ready to unmold.
This has real zing and goes especially well
with beef or ham.

Variation: Stir in a generous amount of cooked,
slivered beets and/or chopped celery at the
point when you add the horseradish mixture.
Use ¾ cup boiling water instead of 1 cup.

## <u>Wine – Raisin Sauce</u> (serves 4)

Especially good with baked ham or tongue (page 112).

<u>3/4 cup seedless raisins</u>, covered with 1/2 cup of the following wine and simmered for <u>5 minutes</u>.

<u>1 cup white wine</u>, Chablis, or champagne, or any white wine.

<u>2 teaspoons corn starch</u>, stirred into remaining half cup of wine along with:

<u>1/4 teaspoon salt</u>
<u>1/4 teaspoon ground cloves</u>
<u>1/4 teaspoon cinnamon</u>
<u>1/2 cup sugar</u>
<u>3 Tablespoons butter</u>

Mix and stir over heat until slightly thickened. Then add the softened raisins and wine.
Serve hot.

## <u>Tartar Sauce</u> (1 cup)
To serve with fish.

<u>3/4 cup mayonnaise</u>
<u>vinegar</u>
<u>chopped sweet pickle</u>
<u>chopped parsley</u>
<u>chopped scallions or onions</u>
<u>capers and/or green olives</u>

1 tablespoon of each mixed into mayonnaise. Chill until ready to serve.

## Dill Carrot Sticks

1 pound carrots — Scrape and cut into 3-inch lengths.
(about 6 medium)   Cook 10 minutes in boiling water. Drain and
cut lengthwise into thin sticks.

3/4 cup sugar
1 cup vinegar
1 cup water
1 tablespoon mustard seed          Simmer 10 minutes in sauce pan
1 teaspoon dried dill weed          (enamel if available). Then
(or heaping tablespoon of fresh chopped)   add carrots and simmer
Salt to taste or skip it!          1 minute more. Cool. Store in
                                   glass jar or jars in refrigerator.
                                   Refrigerate at least 24 hours
                                   before serving either with
cocktails or as a side dish at dinner.
Keeps a long while.

## Lemon-Carrot Relish

To add both color and zest to any meal, this is the ticket.

1 pound carrots, scraped, cut in chunks.   grind in food processor,
1 perfect lemon, washed, cut in pieces    then mix in sugar.
            seeds removed.              Store in glass jar in
                                        refrigerator. (Of course,
                                        an old-fashioned grinder will
1 cup sugar                             do the job also.)

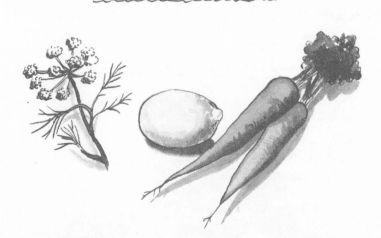

## Iowa Pickled Beets

1 cup cider vinegar
½ cup sugar
½ cup beet water or plain water
½ teaspoon salt
1 one-pound can beets

Bring to boil and pour over cooked beets, sliced or whole. Refrigerate in glass jar. In the simplicity of this recipe lies its goodness.

## Fancy Pickled Beets

1 cup cider vinegar
1 cup beet juice
½ cup sugar
½ teaspoon salt
4 peppercorns
½ bay leaf
½ teaspoon horse radish
1 onion, sliced
1 green pepper, sliced

Bring all this just to a boil and pour over beets that have been placed in a bowl. This recipe is just right for 3 one-pound cans of beets or 12 average garden beets, home cooked. Stir to mix and spoon into 2 one-quart jars. Keep in refrigerator.

## Pennsylvania Dutch Pickled Eggs

Hang onto the juice of either of above recipes and pickle peeled hard-boiled eggs therein. Keep them refrigerated in a glass jar, ready for a picnic or to serve as an hors d'oeuvre.

Dorothy Bryant's    <u>Uncooked Cucumber Pickles</u>

Dorothy was very careful to tell me that this recipe came to her from Mary Smith of Bluffton, South Carolina. A great gift to her, to me.

<u>6 cups thinly sliced, unpeeled cucumbers</u> ✓ About 12 small cucumbers measuring around 4 inches long and 1 inch in diameter.

<u>1½ cups thinly sliced onions</u>, any kind you prefer.
(I use the standard yellow onions that come in a mesh bag. If you're blessed with some Vidalia Onions(!), use those.)

Mix cucumbers and onions in large non-metal container.

<u>2 cups granulated sugar</u>
<u>1 cup cider vinegar</u>
1 teaspoon salt
1 teaspoon <u>celery seed</u>

Mix well and pour over cucumber-onion mixture. Refrigerate for <u>2 days</u> before using, stirring now and then.
Keeps for several weeks in refrigerator. No danger of their lasting too long.

No, nothing is cooked. If the vinegar mixture seems too sparse, the cucumber and onion soon emit their juices, so sufficient liquid develops in which to stir them around. Don't worry about all that sugar, you don't drink the juice.

# Green Tomato Relish (Makes about 2 quarts)

2 quarts green tomatoes, peeled, cut up
    (This takes about 10 or 12 tomatoes, depending on size.)
3 red sweet peppers, centers removed, cut in strips, chopped

3 onions, chopped

1½ cups cider vinegar

1½ cups sugar

1 tablespoon salt

3 tablespoons pickling spice

Place all in a kettle (enamel, if possible). Bring to a
boil and simmer in open kettle until tender and
somewhat evaporated, about ¾ of an hour.
Pour at once into sterile jars and seal.

Kay Teegarden's   Green Pepper Jelly   (8 to 10 jars)

1 1/4 cups chopped green pepper , pressed down, a good full measurement
6 1/2 cups sugar, poured into large kettle.
1 1/2 cups cider vinegar

To chop the peppers even more, place in blender or
food processor with the vinegar and let it whirl.
Pour over sugar in kettle, stir, bring to full
rolling boil only. Remove from heat and
allow to rest for 10 minutes. Then add:

1 bottle (2 packages) Certo

Tabasco , several generous shakes, but be careful!
green coloring, amount according to your artistic eye.

Stir well. Let stand another 10 minutes.
Pour into sterile jelly jars. Seal with paraffin.
Delectable and different.

~~~~~~~~~~~~~~~~~~~~

## Mint Jelly

Make exactly as in above recipe, except no Tabasco.
Instead use a few drops of oil of spearmint, available at most
drug stores. Use 2 cups spearmint leaves, pressed down. Blend
them with vinegar in blender. The green coloring is needed.
This makes a wonderfully assertive jelly, unlike the innocuous
commercial variety.

~~~~~~~~~~~~~~~~~~~~

Midge Crannell's    <u>Peach Jam</u>    (About 12 jelly jars)

<u>9 large peaches</u>, fairly hard but somewhat ripe, over which pour boiling water to loosen skins for peeling. Cut into very thin slices and measure them in quart measure before transferring to large, heavy-bottomed kettle.

<u>Sugar</u>, the exact same measured amount as peaches. Pour onto peaches.

<u>2 large oranges</u>, thick skinned, high grade. Wash skins thoroughly. Cut oranges into chunks and remove all seeds. Then grind them and add to peaches and sugar. <u>Stir.</u> (You may use old-fashioned grinder, being sure to catch the drips, or blender or food processor. Don't make a mush. A little texture is desirable.)

Bring to a <u>full boil</u>, being careful not to scorch. Then turn heat low so peaches just simmer. Let simmer <u>1 hour</u> exactly. <u>Do not cover</u>. Pour into sterile glasses. Add paraffin.

———————

Midge says her husband, Dick, couldn't possibly get through a winter without this jam. Neither can I!

———————

# Three-Day Citrus Marmalade
(Thank you Gretchen Funkhauser Anderson of Nantucket.)

1 grapefruit

2 limes

3 lemons

6 oranges

Choose heavy, perfect, bright-skinned fruit. Wash well.

When it comes to the 6 oranges, try to get 2 each of 3 kinds of oranges:
  2 thin skinned
  2 thick skinned
  2 Temple oranges or tangelos
  (You can even use kumquats)

If varieties of oranges not available use just thin skinned.

**Day 1:** Cut fruit in half and pick out seeds. Place flat side down on cutting board placed in cookie sheet (with sides) and slice fruit as thin as possible with very sharp knife. (Cookie sheet catches juices.) Cut slices into thirds or quarters depending on size of fruit. Transfer fruit and juice to a large enamel (or any non-metal) kettle using quart measure so you know amount you have. Then add twice as much water as you have fruit and juice. Cover and keep in cool place until tomorrow.

**Day 2:** Bring all of above to a hard boil and cook until peel is tender. (Test with fingernails or teeth.) Around ½ hour should do it. Stir often while cooking. When tender, cover and remove to cool place.

**Day 3:** Measure by cupfuls (4 or 6 cups at most) into another cookpot, using ¾ cup sugar to each cup of the juicy fruit. (This step must be done in small batches, so don't try to boil all at once.) Cook each batch to jelly-drop point, about 15 minutes. (Dip out a large spoonful of the marmalade and pour slowly back into kettle. When the last of it settles into two lines of drops which "sheet" together off the edge of the spoon, it is done.) Ladle at once into sterilized jars. Seal and cover at once before doing next batch, being certain to wipe tops of jars clean and dry before sealing.

Gretchen says the foregoing recipe came to her from Amélie Oldham via her daughter, Faith. The making of this marmalade was a holy rite in the Oldham household. "Amélie, a wonderful Swiss woman, used to cut the fruit herself, even when bedridden. She would order Faith around from her second-floor room as the three-day ritual proceeded. Faith kept bringing her samples to test. When Amélie said 'perfect,' the jars were ladled." (I think Faith was wonderful, too, as is this marmalade.)

Don't let the three-day routine scare you off. It is really not that much work, just stretched out in time.

## Houseplant Suggestions

More plants die from over watering than any other cause. Always feel the earth and if it is the least bit moist, don't water.

It is claimed that modern houses are likely to emit a certain amount of toxicity from present-day materials used, such as plywood. The cure for this is simple:
Both spider plant and pothos are said to absorb the toxicity out of house air. These two plants are tough and decorative and do not need watering more than once a week.

Joanne Plantan's    Strawberry Jam (Frozen)

1½ quarts berries, before being hulled
6 cups sugar
2 tablespoons lemon juice
1 bottle Certo — That means 2 pouches
               in a package today.

Hull and crush berries. Add the sugar and lemon and Certo. Mix well and spoon into containers with lids. Let stand for 24 hours. Keep in freezer. (Lids are put on at once, before the 24 hour rest period.)

If you are a collector of the nice little cartons that many products come in, such as sour cream, cottage cheese, oleo, yogurt — use those. Then there are many types of boxes, mostly plastic, that you may purchase. Glass jars are also satisfactory if not filled too full. Allow for expansion.

The freshness of this uncooked jam, on a winter day, makes a memorable treat.

~~~~~~~~~~

## Pear Honey

3 pounds fresh pears, somewhat firm, peeled, cored, cut up fine.
5½ cups sugar
1 eight-ounce can unsweetened crushed pineapple
1 tablespoon lemon juice

Combine all of above in stainless steel or enamelware kettle. Bring to boil over moderate heat, stirring some. Let simmer for 45 minutes or until jam-like. Spoon into sterile jars. Add paraffin.

Remember that anything cooked in enamelware scorches easily.

~~~~~~~~~~

Muriel Manning's **Party Jell** (Serves 8)

I Three-ounce package Peach Jell-O
poured into bowl large enough
for the whole recipe.

2 cups apricot nectar

} Heat 1 cup of apricot juice to a boil and pour over the gelatin, stirring until thoroughly dissolved. Then stir in the remaining cup of cold juice.

I sixteen-ounce can pears
I eight-ounce can pineapple chunks
I eleven-ounce can mandarin oranges

} Drain off all juice and stir fruit into above. Refrigerate to set the jell.

Drink the leftover juices or, better still, save for basting ham.

Once the whole recipe is combined, I put it in my best glass bowl to jell. Then it's all ready to serve. If you prefer to go to the trouble of turning it out of a fancy mold — go ahead. The reason I don't make it all in the good glass bowl to begin with is because the cup of boiling juice might crack the bowl. If you have a heat-proof bowl you're in luck. Nary a dish to wash.

This party jell is a magic mixture with an unidentifiable taste that everyone loves. And it leads a three-way life:
  1. As an accompaniment to meat. (Especially good with ham.)
  2. As a salad
  3. As a dessert

Bets Albright's     **Better Butter**

Bets and her M.D. husband are both into holistic medicine and natural foods to a sensible, not zealous, extent. They use this type of butter exclusively, considering it better tasting and more nature's own product than margarine.

1 pound regular butter, well softened but not heated!

(or 3 sticks regular butter plus 1 stick sweet butter)

3/4 cup safflower, corn or sunflower oil

1 tablespoon lecithin granules, soaked in a tiny bit of warm water. (This is optional but an added plus healthwise.)

Put all this in large beater bowl of electric mixer or into food processor. Let it beat away until thoroughly mixed and smooth.

Transfer mixture to separate ramekins, bowls, cups, whatever. Cover with plastic wrap and keep refrigerated. It is always soft and ready to use. It freezes well. This not only stretches expensive butter but seems to improve it. And it cuts down on cholesterol.

## Heart's Ease "Whipped Cream" (makes 2 cups)

If butterfat is something you avoid for the sake of your heart as well as your waistline, here's your dish.

1 teaspoon unflavored gelatin, placed in a cup
2 teaspoons water, added to gelatin. Let soak about 5 minutes.
3 tablespoons boiling water, poured over soaked gelatin and stirred until thoroughly dissolved
} Allow to cool but not to jell.

½ cup very cold water
½ cup nonfat dry milk
} Combine in the small bowl of mixmaster if you have one, or any small bowl. Refrigerate thoroughly. Then beat at high speed until mixture forms stiff peaks. While still beating, add:

3 tablespoons sugar
3 tablespoons vegetable oil (I use corn oil.)
1 teaspoon vanilla  and last —
the above gelatin mixture
} Beat in well. Refrigerate at once. Cover.

This may be made a day or so ahead and is a very adequate substitute for the whipped cream we all love. It's light, refreshing, delicious and inexpensive.

# Basic Marinade

Concerned about leftover wine languishing in your refrigerator?
Turn it into a marinade, all ready for use.

1 cup wine
1 cup vegetable oil
2 or 3 cloves garlic          Use white wine for poultry or veal.
2 teaspoons rosemary
2 teaspoons thyme
2 teaspoons marjoram          Use red wine for red meats.
1/4 cup chopped parsley
1/2 teaspoon pepper

(For chicken or duck, 1/2 cup orange or pineapple juice is a
pleasing addition.)
Keep marinade refrigerated until ready to use.
Marinate bird or beast, covered, at least 6 hours and up to
24 hours if kept refrigerated. Turn meat in marinade now and then.

# Basic Barbecue Sauce

1 cup molasses
1 cup prepared mustard     Mix and that's it.
1 cup vinegar

# Cranberry Stuffing

This makes enough stuffing for a large crown roast of pork. You may want to reduce recipe to suit your needs. Excellent for stuffing pork chops singly. It should be great with chicken, though I've never tried that.

2 cups cranberries, ground (food processor)
¼ pound butter (1 stick)

} Cook cranberries in butter about 5 minutes in pan large enough for whole recipe. Then stir in

½ cup sugar
8 cups coarse bread crumbs
2 teaspoons salt
¼ teaspoon pepper
1 tablespoon sage (dried)
2 teaspoons thyme (dried)
½ cup chopped celery
3 tablespoons chopped parsley
1 cup water

} Combine all this and add to above cranberry mixture. Stir and cook for 5 minutes or so. Stuffing is now all set to use. (Cool the stuffing before using if its to be in contact with meat for any length of time before cooking.)

This excellent recipe was lost for 20 years — a matter of real frustration. It turned up in the bottom of a filing cabinet. So, cheers, and here it is.

# Sidney's Herb Seasoning

This is a trick I learned in Arkansas from my friend Sidney Nisbet. Not only is she a great artist at her easel, and in her garden, but in the kitchen as well. Here's one of the many things she taught me: to breeze through one's herb collection from start to finish, shaking those of one's choosing into a bowl in quantity desired. And here, roughly, is the usual mix that I come up with:

basil — plenty
bay leaf — a touch
cardamom
celery seed
coriander
curry — careful, not too much
cumin — chives
dill — be lavish
fennel
garlic flakes or powder
marjoram
mustard
onion flakes or powder — in quantity
oregano
parsley flakes — in quantity
pepper
rosemary
saffron — a touch
sage — lots of it
savory, summer and/or winter
sesame
tarragon — plenty
thyme — plenty
a jar of chicken granules
some beef granules
herb blends or herbed salt may be used.

Stir together in bowl, then transfer to blender in manageable loads and blend well. This will keep in tightly covered jar indefinitely. Divide some into small jars as gifts for grateful recipients!

A great way to dust off and use up some neglected herbs. It isn't often that a cupboard cleaning such as this ends in a gustatory delight, but this is that rare exception. I have found this the seasoning without peer for soups that lack authority, for dips, sandwiches, salads, croutons, Melba toast, marinades. Guests are sure to exclaim, "What is it?!" The answer is long in the telling so here it is on paper. Each batch I make differs somewhat. Yours will, too. There are no rigid rules, but this is the nearest I can come to a formula.

Not bouillon cubes! They are too moist. Everything must be dried for long-keeping purposes. These granules give the whole sufficient saltiness.

# X

## Hints and Hangups

Hints — (starting with 3 favorite sayings)

"Order is a lovely thing, on disarray it lays its wing."
(From The Monk in the Kitchen by Anna Hempstead Branch)

"Art is based on order! The world is full of sloppy 'Bohemians' and their work betrays them."
(Edward Weston, great photographer of early 20th century)

"Don't put it down, put it away." (Gladys Elviken)

① Herbs and spices, like prayer, belong in a closet. Be not like the Pharisees and have them on display. Herbs and spices like a dark, cool place. If you can work out a space to keep them in alphabetical order you will save yourself a lot of time and provocation. We all own dozens of them and at the crucial moment can't find the one needed. So its out to the market to buy the missing ingredient, only to discover, later on, that you already had two, fast in the back of some drawer or cupboard. A big "no-no" — herbs and spices in the stove area where they get the two things that destroy their flavor: heat and light.

② If cookies stick to a cookie sheet, place on heat on top of stove and loosen them with spatula as they heat. (Careful not to burn them!) This usually works like magic.

③ To keep ground beef patties on hand always, frozen, is wise. Wrap individually, when fresh from the store, in waxed paper. Store in plastic bag secured with clip clothes pin for easy access. Do not pound the meat cakes into shape. Make them as fragile as possible without their falling apart. Pounded, pressed hamburgers are tough. Don't press them when cooking either. (Almost everyone does.)

④ Don't hesitate to buy a good-sized bunch of bananas. When ideally ripe — peel, wrap, freeze. You are all set for Banana Frappé (page 4 ), Banana Bread (page 213 ) Banana Cake (page 224 )

⑤ Keep a supply of bacon, frozen. It is especially important if you use only a little bacon at a time. Most of us shy away from it these days and it gets too old in refrigerator. The minute brought in from the store, place it, a slice at a time, on the end of a roll of waxed paper. Keep folding over, adding one slice, until each slice is wrapped separately. Then into a plastic bag and into freezer. It only takes minutes. Bacon is always ready, fresh tasting, and not stuck together if you give the package a few minutes at room temperature.

⑥ Don't fry bacon, bake it on foil in oven. The slower the oven, the flatter and more presentable the slices will be. If plenty of time, bake at 250°. If in a hurry, make it 375° to 400°, but watch it! When nicely crisped, remove to paper towel and pat off excess fat. Bacon is more digestible* cooked this way, less work, and no pan to wash (foil lines whatever sized pan needed). Wait for fat to cool (unless you're a bacon-fat saver), wrap up and toss in garbage.

* I didn't make that up. The great Dr. Sara M. Jordan of Lahey Clinic fame told me so.

⑦ Start <u>hot cereals in cold water</u> despite directions to contrary. Why do all directions for cooking oatmeal, corn meal, cream of wheat, etc., say to "pour into boiling water while stirring vigorously"? That way lies lumpy porridge. Pour into cold water and stir casually as it comes to a boil. Never a lump.

⑧ When making <u>white sauce</u> or any sauce or gravy from a roux, <u>always remove the roux from the heat</u> (when flour has cooked sufficiently) <u>before</u> stirring in the liquid. Do that slowly while stirring constantly. Once the liquid is well incorporated and lump-free, return to heat, cook until thickened, stirring pretty constantly. A lump-free creation it will be.

⑨ When boiling <u>corn on the cob</u>, put a dash of vinegar in the water. It makes the corn more tender. <u>No salt!</u>

⑩ When cooking <u>hard-boiled eggs</u>, put some salt in the water. Eggs will peel more easily.

⑪ An <u>avocado pit</u> — leave it in unused half of avocado or in any avocado mixture (until ready to serve). It prevents the avocado from darkening. Plant the magic pit and grow a tree!

⑫ Put a <u>few bay leaves</u> in canisters of flour, or any other product that may get wormy. Bay is a preventative.

⑬ Use <u>real, pure vanilla</u> if you bother to bake. Otherwise don't bother.

14. <u>Roast nuts and seeds</u> for enhanced flavor before adding to a recipe. It makes all the difference with almonds, pecans, macadamia nuts, sesame and poppy seeds, to name a few.

15. <u>Keep well-washed, destemmed parsley</u> in a screwtop jar in refrigerator at all times. It will keep for ages and is so handy for a quick embellishment of almost everything served.

16. Always keep a dish of <u>soft butter</u> in most convenient cupboard ready to grease a pan, butter toast or sandwich. It has countless uses and is also the perfect place to put leftover butter from the table. Hard refrigerated butter can be very frustrating when you're cooking up a storm.

17. When <u>whipping cream</u>, be sure cream, bowl, beater have been <u>well</u> chilled in refrigerator. Speedy whipped cream will be your reward. Don't whack bowl. It takes some of the air out that you've just carefully beaten in.

18. A <u>soup tastes blah</u>? Pep it up with chicken or beef bouillon cube or granules.

19. Don't laugh — <u>always butter a pie plate</u> before pressing in the crust. It's much easier to serve later on.

20. <u>Sift confectioners' sugar</u> when making frosting or hard sauce. It's much easier to banish the lumps if you do.

(21) When a recipe calls for baking soda, its best to sift it with the flour called for. Otherwise it may not mix into batter thoroughly, producing some evil tasting bites in cake, cookie or muffin. (Or rub soda between your fingers and mix it ever so thoroughly into dry ingredients.)

(22) If avoiding fats, whether butter or margarine, make use of bouillon cubes or soy sauce. They give satisfying flavor.

(23) If you can't have salt (which above seasonings contain), use herbs for taste appeal: basil, dill, garlic, lemon, mint, onion, curry, oregano, sage, savory, tarragon, to name a few. The list is long, the choice yours.

(24) Never put very hot cookpot on glass or plastic shelves of a refrigerator. It is tempting to chill soups and such quickly, but don't do it so fast as to crack glass or disfigure plastic. I have, but not any more.

(25) Never freeze a block of ice in any valued or enamel pan. It can wreck them.

(26) Invest in flat skewers for making shish kebabs. Round ones are a nuisance, for when turned, the skewered meat and vegetables have a way of turning also. Not with flat ones. If using disposable wooden skewers, soak in water before using. They do not char as easily. Shish kebabs don't have to be done on an outdoor grill. They do very nicely in the stove, under broiler.

(27) To keep from having a fine fuzz on that half jar of pimiento in the refrigerator, pour a bit of vinegar thereon. It will keep for ages.

(28) Soak badly encrusted pots and pans in a strong solution of water and dishwasher detergent.

(29) There's no better way of getting everything out of the food processor bowl than to use one's bare (clean) hands.

(30) Put rhubarb leaves around to get rid of ants. Rhubarb leaves are, happily, poisonous to ants, but, unhappily, to children (if eaten) also. So watch it.

(31) Don't grieve over a small kitchen. It forces neatness as in a boat's galley.

(32) If you have good linens properly dampened and ready to be ironed and have run out of time, wrap them in a bath towel and refrigerate. They will keep several days this way without molding.

(33) Your good vases getting cloudy, even crusty, with a white lime-like buildup? Soak in vinegar.

(34) Gardening with bare hands? (It's the most fun.) Scratch a cake of soap to fill your nails with same. Then dig in the good earth at will. Wash up with Clorox. To offset chlorine odor, rinse hands in vinegar. Hands and nails will be unscathed, even improved.

(35) Paint on clothing — Equal parts of turpentine and ammonia will remove paint from clothing even if the paint has hardened.

(36) Get yourself to a hotel and restaurant supply store for special needs such as a very large double boiler for parties. They are exciting places, full of sturdy utensils that last forever and are not as expensive as more run-of-the-mill retail stores. You'll see a lot of things the latter don't stock.

(37) Stamps stuck together? Put in a bowl of warm water to soak. They will not run. Dry on paper towels.

(38) Read labels on cans and bottles of foodstuffs. Experts are paid good money to dream up clever ways of using various products. You may come across a jewel of a recipe.

(39) Try to learn to sharpen knives with a steel or stone as butchers do. Because electric sharpeners heat the steel knives they are inclined to remove some of the temper. And oh how valuable is a good knife collection.

(40) Weights printed on various canned and packaged products keep changing. What I have signified last week may have changed this week. Just go ahead bravely, inserting the word "about" before weights indicated.

# Kitchen Imperatives
*(Your list might be different. This is mine.)*

① Clip clothespins in a small basket
within grabbing distance. Mine is on
top of refrigerator. "Twistums" are
time-wasting abominations. Cast them
aside for clothespinclips which can speedily
secure all those plastic bags in refrigerator and elsewhere.
Clips last for years.

② A **French knife** — This is to the Western cook what the cleaver
is to the Oriental. It
will do almost every-
thing a food processor
can, and is often

more convenient when small quantities are involved.

③ **Potato Ricer** — No home was
without this 50 years ago —
and more's the pity if it is today.
They are around, so keep hunting.
Riced potatoes are an easy, delicate treat.
And mashed potatoes made by ricing first are
the best — fluffy, white, nary a lump. A hardboiled
egg, riced, makes a wonderful garnish for salads, soups,
open sandwiches, etc. Easier to do than force through a sieve.

④ **A spreader** — or whatever you call it.

Hard to imagine a kitchen
without one of these. I'd have
trouble spreading a sandwich
without one.

⑤ A kitchen scale — This is an old-timer, that I value, from the Fairbanks Scale Works of St. Johnsbury, Vermont. It was most often found in a candy store in former days, but serves me well in the kitchen. There are plenty of attractive scales on the market and the convenience of your kitchen will be served by having one.

⑥ An egg beater — There's been a subversive movement afoot for some time to replace this handy type of beater with French whisks and electric beaters. Don't be misled. This can be used anywhere in the kitchen without dragging a cord and it will outwhip a whisk every time.

⑦ Ceramic garlic pot — The friend who gave me this garlic pot was shocked that I lacked one. She claims its the only way to keep garlic. She was right. Its decorative, too.
"It is not really an exaggeration to say that peace and happiness begin, geographically, where garlic is used in cooking."
Marcel Boulestin

⑧ A wooden spoon — Most often used in cooking because its light as a feather, the handle doesn't heat up and it won't scratch enamelware and other delicate surfaces. Boulestin, quoted above, waxed lyrical about his favorite cooking spoon. Completely understandable.

⑨ <u>Basic citrus fruit squeezer</u> — How long since you've had a glass of real orange juice a bit thickened with the orange flesh because you haven't strained it out in an electric squeezer, and it isn't bitter because you haven't

pressed out the oil by using the pressure type of squeezer, and there are no seeds because you picked them out with the tip of a spoon? Try it sometime. It can only be achieved with this basic type of squeezer that is getting hard to find. The same goes for squeezing lemons, which I do almost every time I cook. This simple gadget is much easier to wash than those mentioned above. And it produces a flavorful juice that is pure gold.

⑩ <u>Mortar and pestle</u>

A boon for crushing cracker crumbs and herbs.

⑪ <u>Nested cookie cutters</u> — These not only cut cookies in every size, biscuits also, but are even more convenient for dainty open-faced sandwiches. Especially handy for cucumber sandwiches, cutting bread and cucumber slices to match, <u>the</u> welcome tidbit for tea or cocktails.

(12) <u>Dough scraper</u> — Important aid to the bread baker. While dough is still sticky and unmanageable, this does the job of getting it ready to knead by deft scraping up and turning inward! It also cleans up the kneading surface when the job is done.

(13) <u>Metal protector</u> — They come in various forms to prevent scorching by placing on the burner under the cookpot. (Mine is just a triangle of heavy metal wire. There are more substantial varieties, probably

better.) Scorched food can be a catastrophe, so make use of one of these when conditions seem to require it. Aluminum pans are least liable to scorch, stainless steel comes next, enamelware is very scorchable and Corningware is the worst, much as I love it.

(14) <u>Lettuce drier</u> — Maybe this should head the list. No need for wet salads with one of these.

(15) <u>A good bread board</u> — This comes in handy whether you have a butcher block table or not, but is a necessity if you lack a wooden surface to knead bread, make sandwiches and countless other activities. So many kitchens have nothing but a stingy piece of plastic or worse — something with a painted design that gradually gets worked into the food!

⑯ <u>Lid racks</u> ∽ Oh happy day when I found these.

No more hunting for the right lid.

⑰ <u>Hotel can opener</u> ∽ The absolutely foolproof can opener that will handle anything from the tiniest can of sardines to the largest cans of everything. Whither I go it goeth even if I had to install it on a mahogany table. It is called an <u>Edlund</u> can opener and is made in Burlington, Vermont.*

⑱ <u>Double boilers</u> ∽ Be a collector thereof, large and small. They are the secret of cooking without scorching, of reheating in safety, of serving a kitchen buffet that stays hot.

* See next page for how to acquire Edlund can opener.

<u>Edlund can openers</u> are available at restaurant and hotel supply stores all over the U.S.A. Ask for size #2. As of this writing the list price is $37.00. Worth every cent of that for it's a lifetime, foolproof proposition. One needs a sturdy counter or butcher block table on which to install it. If not successful in finding a restaurant/hotel supply place that can provide an Edlund, write or phone: Edlund Company
159 Industrial Parkway
Burlington, Vermont 05401
Phone [802] 862-9661

────────

People often ask me how to get <u>John Cope's Dried Corn</u>. Here's the new address: John F. Cope Co., 156 West Harrisburg Ave., Rheems, Pa. 17570. For three nine-ounce boxes, send $8.00, which includes delivery and handling. Thanks, Betty Williams, for unearthing this information.

────────

As <u>maple syrup</u> is often called for in this book, here's my favorite source: Butternut Mountain Farm, David R. Marvin, Johnson, Vermont 05656. (802) 635-7483 ~ Ever reliable.

────────

You haven't lived unless you've eaten some <u>Vidalia Onions</u>. (Limited availability May through July.)
Bland Farms, P.O. Box 506-G, Glendale, Georgia
30427-9990
They even have a free number: 1-800-843-2542
As of this writing: 10 pounds @ 12.95, 25 pounds @ 29.95

────────

## Entertaining

"The perfect hostess is like a duck,
calm and serene on the surface,
but paddling like hell underneath."
(Anonymous)

There is no form of entertainment that exceeds a small dinner party where good food and good company come together — the highest compliment one can pay a friend. The aim is to send guests home lightly, satisfyingly, healthfully (not heavily!) fed.

If you don't have a fireplace, light candles. "When we can, we should live in rooms with stoves or fireplaces or at least candlelight. The ancient saying is still true: 'Extinguished hearth, extinguished family.'"* Candles should be around anyway in case of power failure, practicality equalling aesthetics. (Save old candle stubs to put in the fireplace to help the fire along.)

When warm weather necessitates the extinguishing of the fireplace fire, put a Boston fern in that forbidding dark place. I learned this trick from my husband's grandmother who created a home of magic in Glenholme, Nova Scotia, nearly 100 years ago. I never knew her, but the nostalgic reminiscences of her many grandchildren indicate that the beauty of the old farm and the table she set made an art form of country living. She always took

---

* All Happy Clans Are Alike by Jane Howard

to the woods in early summer and dug and potted Boston ferns to enhance empty fireplaces. Inspired lady. Her home was ever party-ready and no detail of it ever forgotten.

A cardinal rule I try to follow is never to serve two like things at the same meal. Neither the same foods, the same consistency, even the same colors. This is a discipline, but a good one as it almost guarantees an interesting, tempting, attractive, nourishing, balanced meal.

A few examples of what to avoid:
If you serve cheese with cocktails, don't serve macaroni and cheese with the meal.
If you serve cherry tomatoes for cocktails, don't have a Tomato salad with the meal.
If you have fruit in your salad, don't serve a fruit dessert.
Contrast is everything.

The worst offense is too many creamy dishes at the same meal:
Chicken wallowing in sour cream, along with creamed vegetables and a salad bathed in a rich, creamy dressing, followed by chocolate cream pie topped with whipped cream. Ugh. Don't laugh, this happens, the earnest hostess serving up all her favorite rich dishes at one and the same meal.

With various recipes I've made suggestions as to what I think is appealing as accompaniments. You may not agree, which is fine. Sometimes it helps in planning a menu to have something with which to disagree. (Just as I think it's easier to make over an old house to suit one's wishes than to build a new one.)

Being company-ready means having all food prepared ahead of time, and this book concentrates on that type of cooking. No standing over steaming pots in a hot kitchen while guests wait and wait. There are few soufflés in the book because they demand split-second timing and that can ruin a relaxed atmosphere. People ask, above all, for recipes that are easy for a gang but also delicious and not too cholesterol-inducing. No small order, but I've tried. So that you don't have to paddle too frantically, like the above-pictured duck, on the day you entertain, try to have shopping all done, part of the cooking, and the table all set (its attractive readiness will inspire you) a full day ahead of a party.

Of course some great parties have been given where host and/or hostess manage to get a meal in the midst of guests. Not functioning well that way myself, I bend all efforts toward preparedness.

This quotation by May Sarton says a lot. "One takes so much for granted when one is young! I had never run a house, nor entertained, nor been responsible for ordering meals, and I had no idea what energy it all requires — the devouring machine that someone has to keep running smoothly." And May Sarton is speaking of a household without children, with servants, and of ordering, not cooking the meals. So a gold crown to you young homemakers who do it all, not to mention careers on the side. You are miracle workers.

Probably the greatest boon to the modern host or hostess, without help, is the kitchen buffet. Expend all the creativeness you want on a beautifully set dining table, but then let guests come to the kitchen to help themselves to the good food you have so carefully prepared. In many instances it can be served from the dishes in which it was cooked. No shifting to silver serving dishes. Stove-to-table dishes are the answer and are becoming more attractive every year. Concentrate on collecting them, not forgetting good looking double boilers. Food remains nice and hot served buffet style and guests appreciate the freedom of helping themselves to what they really want. A kitchen buffet saves more work and fetching and carrying than anything I know.

Most old cookbooks have a section confined to remedies for various ailments. Here's a dandy from the 9th Century A.D.

"A drink for a fiend-sick man:

Take cockle, lupine, betony, cockspur-grass, hassock, flower-de-luce, lichen off a church, lichen off a crucifix, and lovage. Place all in clear ale. Sing seven masses over the mixture, put in garlic and holy water, and drip drops of this into every drink which the patient takes. Let him sing the psalms Beati immaculati and Exsurgat and Salvum me fac, Deus, and then let him drink of this drink, from a church bell. After he has drunk, let the priest sing over him Domine, Sancte Pater Omnipotens."

(From Bald's Leechbook, perhaps put together under the inspiration of Alfred the Great. Alfred the Great by Eleanor Shipley Duckett University of Chicago Press.)

Does this make you want to go back to the "good old days"?

# A Peek Into a 21st Century Kitchen

(From a study by 14 national experts, funded by the Whirlpool Corporation.)

Single people will comprise about 35% of all U.S.A. households.
Almost all people will eat at least half of their meals outside the home.
Most at-home meals will be purchased fully prepared, hence:
  Very little counter space, few ovens, microwave ovens standard in all homes.
Food irradiation will make freezers obsolete and refrigerators will be small
  and needed mostly for ice and chilled drinks.
Everything from milk to fish will be stored in cupboards.
Kitchen and dining room will be combined as one "great room" that
  will be an entertainment and operations center with laser disks,
  cable T.V., electronic shopping and banking, security control,
  and appliance control.
Most tasks will be programmed in the morning and completed while
  one is at work.

What would Harriet Beecher Stowe say to all this?! Here's what she had to say about the iron cookstove of the 19th century (that we consider so romantic) replacing fireplace cooking: "An open fireplace is an altar of patriotism. Would our Revolutionary fathers have gone barefooted and bleeding over snows to defend air-tight stoves and cooking ranges? I trow not. It was the memory of the great open kitchen-fire ... that called to them through the snows of that dreadful winter."

One wonders whether the microwave oven will inspire future generations to high sacrifice. I only know that the ways of cooking presented in this book will seem as quaint in the 21st century as the remarks of Harriet Beecher Stowe do here and now.

306

<u>American Heritage</u> magazine ran an article not long ago with answers by famous people to the question, "<u>At what moment in history would you like to have been present?</u>" They didn't ask me but I have an answer ready:

Oh to have been present in the early 1800's at a meal-planning session between the great statesman Charles Maurice de Talleyrand-Perigord, that "epicure of the table as well as other pleasures", and Antonin (Marie-Antoine) Carême, "the Cook of kings and the King of cooks" Talleyrand's esteemed chef of many years. Carême's exquisite cooking caused the royalty of Europe to vie with one another for his services. The perfectionism and imagination of both men concerning matters of food has never been excelled. The very thought of being on hand at one of their counsels really "sends me."

"Cookery [has been called] the most selfless of all the arts because the least enduring. A bite or two, a little gulp and a beautiful work of thought and love is no more."* But the <u>memory</u> endures. And what can exceed in importance good memories? I have lots of those and wish the same to the reader. And as a parting shot concerning age which hurries on apace:

Be of good cheer. Granted the blessing of good health, one can find the most sugar in the bottom of the cup.

*Sybil Ryall

# Index

310

313